Adam Hamilton Leppere

**The Rainbow Creed**

A Story of the Times

Adam Hamilton Leppere

**The Rainbow Creed**
*A Story of the Times*

ISBN/EAN: 9783744677882

Printed in Europe, USA, Canada, Australia, Japan

Cover: Foto ©Thomas Meinert / pixelio.de

More available books at **www.hansebooks.com**

# THE
# RAINBOW CREED.

"........ shame."
*....ing's Prometheus.*

Entered according to Act of Congre.
ADAM HAMILTON,
In the office of the Librarian of Congress at Washington.

# PREFACE.

WHY do ye speak, O writer bold, so lightly of sacred things?

Please read the book, and if you find therein unseemly mirth, burn it, lest another suffer harm. Vice puts a fool's hat on Superstition's head, and Religion herself invites us to deride the follies of the day, even as in olden time she made Elijah laugh at the priests of Baal. It is true the latter are no more, but those of Mammon now are at the altars, and it might be well to mine their temples. There is a dearth of soul: and of love we feel a woful lack. We long for a prophet to bring their subtile influence, not from the fountains of the skies, but from those that have their source within.

Who can escape the evils of the day?* The infection

---

* "The last article in The New York Intelligencer by James Anthony Froude considers the Causes of Weakness in Modern Protestant Churches. 'But Protestant nations have been guilty, as nations, of enormous crimes. Protestant individuals who profess the soundest of creeds seem, in their conduct, to have no creed at all beyond a conviction that pleasure is pleasant, and that money will purchase it. Political corruption grows up; sharp practice in trade grows up; dishonest speculations, short weights and measures, and adulteration of food. The whole commercial and political Protestant world, on both sides of the Atlantic, has blossomed out into transactions of this kind, and the clergy have for the most part sat by silent, and occupy themselves in carving and polishing into completeness their schemes of doctrinal salvation. They shrink from offending the wealthy members of their

from indigent homes ascends the slopes of Beacon Hill, and, baffling the efforts of the best physicians, desolates the most luxurious ones. What did Louis Napoleon win for self when all was done? Therefore shut not, O man of superior advantages, the doors of thy heart, and lock them with the key of conventional Religion, nor even those of thy house, on whose threshold servile Fashion too often stands to keep salvation out. Seest thou not the bridge which spans the gulf that separates the hovel from the palace, and, hark! hearest thou not a tramping upon it, the tramping of the troops of Death? Behold the word on their banners, — "FRATERNITY;" and that which is written on their blades, — "JUSTICE." This ghastly throng passes hither and thither, and naught can stay its terrible power but one simple thing, — and that is to let our greatness lie in nearness to, not in distance from, the suffering men below. Distress is fuel to feed the flame of Love. For what can Heaven be but the cure of Hell? The Most High live, and, if need be, die, for the good of those beneath them; and it is this operation of the Holy Spirit of Goodness, as possessed by them, which constitutes the glory of God and the true Vicarious Atonement.

congregations. They withdraw into the affairs of the other world, and leave the present world to the men of business and the Devil. — *Boston Transcript*, April 2, 1873.

# BOOK I.

## MALCOLM LAWSON AND ORA-TONE BUZZ.

# I.

## GENESIS AND EXODUS.

*"Dulcia non meruit, qui non gustavit amara."*

JEAN PAUL says, "The origin of a man is as dark as his disappearance; the best time to sow is when thick fogs prevail." This brings before us the familiar fact that the life of an upright man is a clear gain to the world, and allows us to infer that he is the fruit of a seed sown by the inscrutable Source of Thought in the muddy yet fertile soil of earthly existence, — which fruit is not to be classed with its husk, but to receive treatment according to its value. The aspect of the difficulties which beset the culture of this fruit, especially in the fields of theology, where we have had some experience, has induced us to sketch a scene or two from the life of a student called Malcolm Lawson. If, then, the reader will follow us into a fine house, in the good city of Bragville, he shall hear him tell his intended bride about his early childhood and youth.

"I lived with my step-brothers till I was ten or eleven years old. We often quarreled with one another, and even had recourse to the fist to arbitrate between us. I am sorry to say that I was as bad as the rest. But many of the neighbors thought I was the most mischievous of the lot; and, to tell you the truth, appearances were sadly against me, and greatly in favor of the others. My brothers were always so neat and dignified, and my sister was rather prim. What piles of Sunday-school tickets they had! They never ran off alone into the woods, and sought, to the serious injury of their brown linen pinafores, the nests of the magpie and hawk; nor forgot the dinner-hour in listening to the wild tales of the Celtic fishermen who mended their nets on the shore within sight of the pigmy thatched cottage that we called home. Nor did they scamper off and hide, when the old village minister dropped in, lest they should be called in to regale the ears of the household with a hymn or a part of a psalm. No: such nice, pious children as they appeared to be were not likely to be in the wrong, while I, who plead guilty to all those crimes, was termed an uncanny changeling. That, you must know, is the miserable substitute of the fairies for the rosy, plump child which they steal from the new-made mother. I probably got the name from my solitary disposition, being often found, even after sundown, in the haunted spots of the neighborhood. And the more superstitious, connecting with this peculiarity the difficulty I had in learning by heart my weekly portion of Scripture which was dealt out to us,— as Mrs. Squeers dosed the unwilling urchins of Dotheboys Hall with sulphur and molasses,— hinted that I was not a fit companion for the more apt scholars, who, however, profited so little by their instruction, that, the moment the teacher's back was turned, they did not scruple to pounce upon his early strawberries and other horticultural delicacies."

"The little hypocrites!" exclaimed Jennie.

"But the difference between me and the other children," continued Malcolm, "was essentially one of races, my mother being a pure Celt, while theirs was a Scandinavian, like my father and the most of the neighbors. I naturally took after my Highland forefathers, who loved the freedom of the forest and the heath, while my brothers inherited an aptitude for trade and other practical abilities that characterize the Scandinavian element in Darkland. This fact was far beyond the reflection of the place, and I had to suffer for my exceptional character."

"But your mother — did she not take your part?" asked Jennie.

"My poor mother died when I was little more than a baby. All I remember of her was the pale face which hung over my crib in a frame of dark brown hair, and the sweet voice which sung me to sleep when I had grown tired of playing with a curl, or of looking up into two deep black eyes."

"And your father?" asked Jennie again, with a less confident voice.

"He was a changed man, they told me, from the hour of my mother's death. His grief was deepened by the consciousness that he might have been kinder to her. His other children having induced him to share their natural prejudice against their step-mother, he had to suffer for his want of discrimination. He died several years afterward.

Here Malcolm paused, and appeared lost in thought. The ready sympathy of the maiden came to his aid. She took his hand, as if to assure him that she was there to compensate him for his bereavements, and asked what he did after his father's death.

"Oh, pardon me," he replied, bethinking himself, "I was about to say, that, as father left us without property, we were thrown on the kindness of relatives, and obliged to conform to their will. Having come to the funeral, they held a consultation in regard to our future. A good-humored uncle, to my great joy, adopted my sister; a friend fancied my brothers, who gladly went off with him; and I was left alone in the care of my grandmother, the only surviving relative on my mother's side. She was very kind to me; and, content to share her humble fare, quite happy in her sympathetic and instructive society, I staid in Cathorm till I was fifteen. During all this time I was in the garden of Eden. It is true, thorns and thistles grew there as well as elsewhere, but they were not thorns and thistles to me; or, if they were, I was one of themselves, rejoicing in the same sunshine, in the same delightful air, taking no thought for the morrow, having no consciousness of want. I toiled not, neither did I spin, yet his Royal Highness the Prince of Wales, in all the splendor of his court, could not have been happier than I. But this was not to last forever. The angels came at length, and, with fiery swords in hand, drove me from my paradise."

"Angels of Darkness, you mean!" exclaimed the young lady.

"Yes, indeed," replied Malcolm. "I had to yield to Death and Necessity. They showed no mercy, and I was thrust out of my ignorant but happy indolence, and made to work for a living. Nor do I regret it, now that I think of it," he added, reflectively; and, indeed, he had no cause, considering that, after being fitted to enjoy it by his experience in the thorny region without, he had obtained a different Eden, and a fair Eve into the bargain.

"My grandmother," he went on, "fell ill, and died. Her loss was far more painful than either my father's or mother's; for I had grown old enough to realize all that she had been to me. Having been herself alone in the world, the last daughter of a once powerful family, she had lavished the full wealth of her affection upon me. She had always received me with open arms when I ran to pour into her ready ears the tales of my childish woes. She never had spoken a harsh word to me, although I am conscience stricken at the thought of how much occasion I must have given her. Her last crust had been shared with me, her last prayer had been made for me, and her last breath had blessed me. My childish heart was frozen by this, my greatest calamity. I was stupefied by sorrow. Not till the gates of the tomb were closed upon her clay did I obtain relief. Then the plaintive dirge of the Celtic mourners, who followed it thither, thawed my heart, and I was flooded with grief."

A tear of sympathy glistened on the cheek of the

young lady, who, having some years before lost her own mother, realized only too well how he must have suffered. Malcolm saw it, and continued his story in a tone less sad.

"Cathorm could no longer remain my home. For the first time it appeared bleak, frigid, inhospitable. All its brightness and beauty seemed to have departed with my late friend. But a nameless attraction made me linger amid the scenes of past happiness. Yet, having no means of support in this remote region, I had to go to a Scotch friend in the south, who offered me a situation in his counting-house. I was kindly received; and for a while amused by the change, and impressed by the grandeur of a city, I was not unhappy. But, reaction soon coming, I pined for my old home in the north, and became foolishly discontented. I only perceived, without being able to realize, the propriety of exerting myself to excel in my present vocation, in order to find the solacement I required. Therefore I could not but dislike it together with other circumstances of my sojourn there. The city itself, which I had admired so much at first, became a confused mass of fog-and-soot-begrimed brick and stone,— a species of labyrinth in which an evil genius held me captive. How I wished for wings, and other impossibilities, that I might escape from its dust and din, and fly to the purple hills where I had listened to the bleat of the wandering sheep and the wail of the plover! And how I longed for my nooks among the cliffs, where I had sat and rejoiced with the sea-birds that speckled the sky overhead, watching the big billows come towering in from afar to worship, with fanatic zeal, their lofty gods of stone, and lay at their feet the treasures of the deep,—endless heaps of sea-weed and shells! My friends soon saw that something ailed me, and did their best to console me in their own way. But in vain.

"A mountain goat will not fraternize with southdown sheep. The people and the place were alike good, yet I had little pleasure in either. An oppressive melancholy stole in upon me, which, together with my native fogginess, made me the butt of my companions, and did not add to my usefulness in the office. I sometimes felt that I belonged to a necropolis, and the desk was the coffin to which I was obliged to hurry at cock-crow. To give you some idea of how I then was, I'll tell you a dialogue that I overheard, between my employer and a friend relative to my merits. The former, in answer to the question how he liked me, said, 'I canna make heed or tail of the lad. He's always dreaming about something or 'ither that has no more to dae wi' his work than the mon in the moon. He's not good for muckle here.' 'Why, is the boy stupid?' asked the friend. 'No, I cannot say he's stupid,' replied my employer: 'he's kind of *dopit*. He daes things as if he did not care whether he did them or no. The boy is more like a bogle than anything else. Where do you think I found him the other nicht, as I was comin' hame frae Tam's?' 'I can't say.' 'Weel, as I was comin' along on the far-awa' side of the auld kirkyard, aboot twelve o'clock,—it is awfu' lonesome doon among yon tall, naked firs, mind ye, and I walked pretty middlin' quick, as I dinna like to stop in sic places any longer than I can help,—I heard a maist unearthly singin'. A cauld chill cam' over me, and I stopped as if somebudy had knocked me on the heed. I was just about to take to my heels, when I thocht I kenn't the voice. Pluckin' up my courage, I walked up to the dyke, and keeked over,—and whom dae you think I saw? Our Malcolm: there he sat, astraddle of auld McBride's tombstone, singin' ane o' they wild Highland songs of his, carin' no more about the bogles than an auld hen just gone to roost. "What are you daein' there?" says I to him. He stopped the singin', and, turnin' round his heed, he saw it was I, and said, jumpin' down and walkin' up to me, "A fine nicht, Mr. Donald." "Weel, Malcolm," says I, "this is a queer place to be this time o' nicht." "Oh," says he, "I could na sleep, so I cam' out to get a sicht of the moon through the ruined arches of the auld abbey." "And did you never see a bogle?" says I. "Plenty of them," says he, and he walked home to the city, as if he had been to a *soirée* at the kirk.'"

"You saw no ghosts!" exclaimed the conscientious Jennie.

"Yes, I did," he replied, decidedly, yet with rather a sad look.

Jennie was puzzled; but on his adding that he often felt that he was something of a ghost himself, she caught a glimpse of his meaning.

"Yes," he continued, with an absent air: "it has

occurred to me more than once that I was only a spectre, obliged to appear, for some mysterious reason, during a brief period in the masquerade which some call Life, and then to vanish, with or without the object of my coming, which," he added, with a smile, " may be only a dance with a suitable partner or the opposite."

"Only a dance!" repeated his companion, a shade of vague fear passing over her young face.

"Yes, only a dance, and often a horrible one; for, as I whirl in its mazes, I see the life-flush of beauty strangely blend with the ghastly pallor of the dead."

"Nonsense!" exclaimed Jennie: "all that comes of riding on McBride's tombstone. If you continue in that strain you will frighten me away. Already you have sown in my mind the seeds of dreadful dreams."

"I beg pardon, Jennie. But was it surprising, seeing how few friends I had amongst the living, that I sought the society of the mystic dead, no, not dead, yet" —

Here he paused, and Jennie replied, "Perhaps not, but don't talk about them any more to-night. Wait till next Sunday, when Dr. Pluffle will be here. He will be sure to sympathize with you." And she finished with a sly look.

"No doubt," returned Malcolm, who did not relish the suggestion, "he is sepulchral enough to sympathize with a graveyard turned inside out."

At her request to tell her more about himself, he continued: "That encounter with my master was only one of the many instances which satisfied my friends that I would never make a merchant. What were they to do with me? So far as they could see, I was fit for nothing under the sun, but singin' Highland songs and ridin' on tombstones. There was no end to the jokes I had to suffer for that moonlight exploit of mine. 'We maun leave him to Providence,' they wisely concluded, and so I was left to the watchful supervision of that Being. This was the best thing that could have happened to me. I grew all the better for being thus thrown on the rocks. Adversity, luckily, is a she-wolf. My romantic disposition impelled me to go to sea, or indeed anywhere to escape the bondage of trade. Going to sea was the most feasible thing. I made what little preparation I could, and, one bright October morning, took my traps in one hand, and kissing the other to the gilt clock of the steeple opposite, about the only thing I learned to like, I stole down to the quay, where I was not long in making terms with a captain; and in a fortnight I was a thousand miles on my way to Hong Kong."

"And you found this a change for the better?"

"In some respects," he replied. "For the first few days, as long as we remained on smooth water, within sight of charming shores, I liked it much. But when we got out to sea I had a far different experience. Not that I cared about the transient sea-sickness and the hard work: but my companions were ignorant, and even brutal. To recall my early life in the forcastle is to bring Dante's Inferno before me. I will not dwell upon it. Yet on deck I was happy. I enjoyed the ever-changing face of heaven, and even liked what the other sailors abhorred, — the furling of the royals. My willingness to undertake this fatiguing duty made them friendly to me. The continued exposure did me good, and I thrived in every physical respect, though, if you had seen me, anointing the rigging, a bucket of tar dangling from my neck, seated in the loop of rope called a boatswain's chair, you would not have thought me handsome. But I learned to call it a throne, seeing" —

"I thought you disliked a seaman's life, all things considered."

"I would not gladly return to it. Thrones are properly termed thorny seats. I worked hard to resign my sceptre, a marlin-spike, if you please, and my crown, the sou'-wester. But there was no usurper at hand, — and on this account I slept better than most kings."

"Yet you succeeded at last, it seems."

"Yes: I soon saw that unless I exerted myself to throw aside my insignia, I should suffer from the burden, like all rulers. Therefore I labored for a less onerous task. I talked with foreign sailors, learned more or less of their language, devoured an odd grammar or two, swallowed a dictionary, washing it down with novels, and so forth. And, though I suffered from ensuing indigestion, I recovered at last. I was bound to learn something; and, becoming feverish, my appetite for knowledge increased, and I had to gratify it as I best knew. The world bent to my will, acknowledging the legality of my self-assumed title, and I had more than enough tribute paid me. And now you come, or rather I come to you, from afar. I tell you the human will is inscrutable,—a direct emanation from the Source of all Power, even in the bosom of the lad who is swept by a pitiless wave from the helm of a coaster."

## II.

### THE MERCHANT PRINCE.

> "The nations' Life upon their bonds depends,
> The blood wherein Disease with Health contends.
> To head and heart too much is apt to course,
> And thus the other portions lose their force.
> Therefore intestine strikes and wars arise,
> Which some destroy, and others paralyze."
> — *J. Sweep.*

THOMAS CRISP was a most respectable man. Born of poor Huberton parents, he had at an early age emigrated to the West, and quickly grown in opulence with the place which had become his home. Taken altogether, he was not a bad type of New Humbleton shrewdness in business matters, and of mental mediocrity in every other respect. A little more than conventionally religious from the first, he placed his trust in the Lord, as well as in his surplus balance, and thus far never regretted the division in his faith. He was now situated like Job, before that unhappy man had been plagued by the Devil. A kind fate was pouring into his lap the horn of plenty, and he sat portly, complacent and pious, thoroughly enjoying the spectacle of his prosperity.

But was Mr. Crisp really a Christian? He thought so, being the flattered favorite of his denomination, which finds such men uncommonly useful. Either that or the native vanity of our old friend persuaded him that he was eloquent, and he lost no opportunity of displaying his imagined gift. His religious friends had made him president of the great Continental Miracle Protection Association, and it was a satisfaction to see him in the chair thereof. How evangelical his presence, how vehement his tone, as he rose and denounced this infidel age, and threatened it with the fate of Sodom and Gomorrah if it did not repent and stand up for the Lord !

His prophetic eye probably foresaw the recent conflagrations, but realizing the overwhelming power of his avenging God and the feebleness of all human resistance thereto, he did not think it worth his while to prepare the fire department for those calamities. Nor did it ever occur to him, until he saw his cherished properties disappear, that Mansard roofs provoked the appetites of fiery dragons. Therefore Mr. Crisp maintained with *éclat* his social position as a defender of the Faith.

His enthusiasm in the cause of homely morality, before which the word "mere" is often prefixed, never equaled his zeal for the propagation of his religion. Yet he could not be called a hypocrite. He was simply one of those well-known beings, sometimes termed Pharisees, who are so permeated by the odor of respectability and sanctity that few detect that of their worldliness and sin, be these either past or present. Many years ago Mr. Crisp had speculated in whiskey, and that with signal success. This fortunate event gave him the needed start, and laid the corner-stone of his opulence, which was gradually built up by industry and skill. But these were assisted by a mysterious and lucrative connection with some doubtful railroad companies and land-grabbing enterprises. However, we must remember the character of the present time, and not erect too high a standard for the judgment of such pioneers as Mr. Crisp, who do so much to develop the resources of the country and extend the empire of Christianity.

To atone for his peccadillos, he now devoted much time and money to the service of his Maker. Not merely interested in the conversion of Pacific Islands, he also subscribed liberally to various home charities, especially to all schemes for dispensing the Gospel to the poor. Standing midway between the old and new Schools of Theology, he did not object to free churches, and on one occasion gave ten thousand dollars toward the erection of a steeple two hundred and fifty feet high, — "an act of beneficence," the new sexton warmly remarked, "which would carry his name down to remote posterity." While we gazed upon this wonderful piece of modern architecture, an irreverent companion hinted something about Midas, saying the deacon had done more to enlarge his purse than his mind. We could only hope that the fullness of the former, in addition to his faith in the Lord, would compensate him for the deficiencies of the latter.

His only child, Miss Jennie, presided over his splendid establishment in Upper Tenth Avenue. She inherited from her late mother a fine disposition and intellect, and owing to these, rather than external advantages, she shone brightly among her companions.  Her generous spirit and loving nature disarmed the envy excited by her superior beauty and attainments.  Yet she did not escape entirely uninjured by those evil influences which, lurking in the best society, sometimes spoil the most promising characters.  Superstition, Flattery, and the frivolities of Fashion combined to darken her mind and interfere with her enjoyment of Life.  She was like a rare and beautiful plant surrounded by weeds, which, while they shield it from the storms and the hot sun, interfere with its growth and make the blossoms small.  Her father idolized her and gave her all she desired, from the finest pictures and jewels to trips to Europe and California.  Yet, not content with all those blessings, the perverse child, to the indignation of her affluent parent and the astonishment of the world, fell in love with a poor young man, and, with a strength of will previously unsuspected, insisted on having him for a husband In him you may recognize the Malcolm of the preceeding chapter.

# III.

## A SLAVE-KING.

NEXT evening Malcolm resumed his story to Jennie, while the deacon lay half asleep on the sofa.

"I soon saw that, if learning was gold, my mind was a bank; so I got books, and increased my thought. And I believe now that, if I had not been bondsman to my body, I would have grown infinitely rich."

"No wonder, then, you thought yourself a king; for a king, according to the original Saxon, is one who *can* or knows. Besides, the Kingdom of Heaven being within, it was natural for you to lay up treasures there. But that is not all. Sou'wester and spike may do for crown and sceptre, but how about your subjects?"

"Oh, men both in and out of my books, these were my subjects, — prophets, kings, queens, ambassadors. Peter the Great was a ship carpenter: I was a sailor."

"But you could not always feel so, Malcolm?" asked the wondering girl, recalling Dr. Pluffle's morning sermon on "What is man that thou art mindful of him?"

"Alas, no. Circumstances conspired against me, and the tides of Fate came rolling down upon me; but I bore up, and thus made head against the seas.

A castaway once on the African coast, I helped to bury twenty comrades in the precious sands, I being one of three surviving; the shrunken inmate of a pest-house, I moaned for months; lost in the woods of Borneo, I wrestled with wild beasts; and, what was worse by far, I had to herd with devils. But even if I shared I did not yield to the pangs of the doomed. I lived on, hopefully, and, when I had no love for my kind, I had some for the parrot that shared my wormy bread, and for the seas that battered the walls of my castle."

"How strange, Malcolm! You make me think of Epictetus, the slave of slaves, yet a king of kings. How wild the paradox!"

"Not so strange, either! You forget that the past was mine, and the future, too; and the stars told me that I was richer than they. And the sun, did he not come to fill my coffers with gold, brighter far, yet infinitely less burdensome, than that of Ophir? And each day, was it not the blessing of God? What more did I need? I had an eye, and I beheld the universe; and it was this simple thought that made me worthy of the splendors I saw, and brought me safe to thee, fair queen of my heart!"

"Heart, heart!" echoed the deacon, waking and putting on his glasses as he arose, "surely, children, you are not playing cards to-night?"

"Don't fear, papa," cried his child, blushing; "Malcolm was telling me about a king and a queen who lived in an air castle."

"Was he? But positively, children, I am astonished that you should not be engaged more profitably. Is that all the good those splendid words of Dr. Pluffle have done you? Man, man, thou art but little indeed, when all is said and done. If such as Paul can call himself 'the offscouring of all things unto this day,' who are we that we should plume ourselves on our reason and our intelligence? O my children, be not misled by the false images of a deceitful imagination."

"But, dear papa, don't you believe in poetry?"

"Why, yes, my dear; I am never tired of Dr. Watts and the Hymns of the Spirit. But, in regard to profane writers, I have not seen a verse for an age except a few of Sir Walter Scott's. By the way, it is a pity that even Christian men of genius should turn away from the religious side of life to occupy themselves with the purely secular."

"I can't say," said Malcolm, "that I admire Sir Walter. What he writes may be worth reading, but it is never worth quoting. He was too fond of real estate to be spiritually great."

"'Too fond of real estate'!" repeated Mr. Crisp with deliberation; "what in all the world do you think a man can do without real estate? I presume you prefer the luxurious life in the castle of that air-king of yours to our poor city fare here?"

"Sometimes I do, and sometimes I don't. I admired dissolving views of the world; and, although I had to put up with much evil, I never, in any one place, saw more of 'the offscouring of all things' than is heaped up in Bragville here. But custom, they say, dulls the sense; and I suppose if I go, as you wish, to a divinity school, I will learn to take it as easy as the best of them."

"God forbid, Malcolm, that you should lose the sense of man's lost condition without a Divine Saviour. Do not misunderstand me. I only sought, in my blunt way, to prune your rather luxuriant imagination."

"Oh, papa!" cried Jennie, "you are too critical. After all, Malcolm's castles in the air may be as real as your mansions in the skies."

"Jennie, Jennie!" cried Mr. Crisp, severely. "This is the fourth time to-day I have had occasion to blame you for misuse of sacred words. I must insist on your being more careful in future."

The conversation being over for the evening, let us give our version of Malcolm. A student even under the most adverse circumstances, he had labored to fit himself for a teacher in some school; and, when he thought he knew enough, he left his ship and tried to find a situation in the East; but not succeeding he went West, and labored according to season and opportunity. In summer he would work in the fields, or take voyages on the great lakes; in winter he did whatever he could find to do. Yet, no matter what happened to him, he never forgot himself or his King-ship, as he playfully called it; for he loved the world, and, if he could not teach it, he was glad to have it teach him. It is now the same with the son of man as it has ever been: "The foxes have holes, and the birds of the air have nests;" but it sometimes happens that he has not "where to lay his head."

# IV.

### AN ITEM IN SATAN'S TAX-BILL.

ONE Autumn Malcolm sailed on board a lake steamer. During a dark and stormy night, it happened to come into collision with another, and thereby sustained so much damage that it threatened to sink in an hour. Fortunately the more faulty boat escaped with little or no injury, and, apprehending at once the full extent of the disaster, lowered her boats as quickly as the ugly weather permitted, and sent them to the rescue. Meanwhile great confusion prevailed in the sinking vessel, which now carried her full complement of passengers. These, roused by the concussion, awoke in terror, and, pouring frantically on the decks, neutralized, in their anxiety to save and be saved, the efforts of the captain and crew. In their natural but selfish struggle for places in the boats, they swept discipline aside, and, crowding in, swamped them almost the moment they were launched. During this time the fury of the tempest increased, and the darkness thickened, to the hindrance of those who were coming to the rescue.

What a change! The mighty ship, the floating city, which but a few seconds ago so proudly defied the forces of the deep, now lies at their mercy.

The cavalry of the sea shake their plumes of foam, and, shooting their arrows of spray, rush tumultuously upon her; and their forms have a ghastly sheen in the blue lights of the lamps. They ride with a roar, and break with a crash on the powerless walls; and the noise of the charge, rising above the din of the steam, and mingling with that of the storm, drowns the shriek of distress and the word of command. It is an hour of awe and sickening suspense. Many have perished in the boats. Young wives and husbands are there, and, dropping the cup of their first connubial joy, they stand in dismay over the fragments. Fathers and mothers are there, and they know not what to do in this terrible gloom. Faint with anguish, or wild with fear, they press their babes to their breasts, or seek, with unspeakable woe, the means of possible safety, while children weep, and cling to their knees, or dolefully hang on their skirts. The superstitious are the first to despair, and, clasping their hands, they pray for the help which only can come with the exertion of muscle and brain. And some, overborne by sleepy resignation, the ether God-sent at the prospect of Death, gaze upon the appalling surroundings in stupid bewilderment, while the valiant few attend to the remaining boats, which are soon safely launched, and freighted with valuable life.

"Hurrah! the boats have come!" is the thrilling intelligence. "But is there time to save us all?" is the fearful doubt which sinks, like a javelin, into the hearts of those who remain. For, although the boats have come, and are being filled with a grateful throng, there is not a moment to waste. The bow of the ship is ominously depressed, and the foe is master of most of the decks. Alas! there is not time to save them all. Another minute is gone from the Earth, and several are left to a watery tomb. The irresistible forces of the deep sweep over the steamer, — but one more faint cry from a vortex of waves, and the trouble and woe of a number are past. The elements are left in possession of the city they surprised, and they still roar on with fury unabated.

Malcolm staid on the ill-fated ship to the very last, as he could not bear to leave the helpless without aid. But the instant his practised eye detected that the boats, if they valued their safety, would soon be obliged to sheer off, he endeavored to get into one, and was in the act of reaching it, when an old gentlemen, whom some accident had lamed, besought his aid. The youth did not hesitate a moment, and, exerting himself, succeeded in helping him into the boat, yet not without mishap to himself. He lost his balance, while standing on the gunwale, and, falling into the sea, would surely have perished, had he not caught a rope which providentially hung from the stern. No swimmer could hope to live in the terrible billows.

This was one of those frightfully frequent accidents due to the want of "mere morality." The man on the look-out had allowed his vision to be obscured by drink. Yet how can the ignorant authors of the distress thus entailed upon us be blamed? Hear the words of Jeremiah Sweep on this subject: "Art thou, O world, to be a perpetual martyr to thine own cant and foul indifference? Withdraw thy vision from the vacant skies, and fix it upon thyself. For thou hast prayed sufficiently long to the fictions of thy distempered brain, to the dim illusions of thy present ignorance and undevelopment. Thou hast still a heart. Make haste and call upon the Loving Spirit who dwelleth therein for the salvation thou requirest, and the gates of Heaven will open at once, and thou shalt enter and be filled with new Life. For thine is the kingdom, the power, and the glory for the taking. Canst thou not see with some of thy two billion eyes that thy Satan is the attorney of God, the unanswerable advocate of good on the negative side? How long must he be hired to teach thee the simple truth that true prosperity can only come with self-help? Read his argument in the dismal panorama of all thy suffering, which clearly demonstrates the falsity of Fraud, and the truth of Honesty. And weigh well the exorbitant fees he obtains. For these consist in thy actual suffering itself, the coin of unsightly disease and untimely death, the desolation of thy cherished cities and fields. O star-gazing and phantom-hugging world, notwithstanding all thy free speech and boasted emancipation from the authority of kings, thou art little better than the nation of frogs that elected a stork to be its monarch. Behold thy Vices. These are thy rulers, and what tax bills theirs!

# V.

## A FAVORED ONE.

THE gentleman whom Malcolm saved proved to be Mr. Crisp, who, when he was himself again, said to Malcolm, "You have saved my life, young man, and I must acknowledge the service."

And Malcolm replied, "I am used to the sea, sir, and must do just so, or become worse than useless. I am part of my ship, and, like a rope or a mast, must endure till I give way. You owe me nothing."

"Do you call my life nothing?" and the deacon cast a crushing look on some young men who had been saved, and were now playing poker. "Believe me, I wish to help you. Here, take this. I know by your face that you will not waste it; and it is no loss to me."

"No, thank you, sir, I'd rather not;" and he blushed.

"What, so poor, and refuse an honest thousand?"

"I am not ungrateful, sir. It is true that I am poor; yet I am better off than you think. All men have served me, and must I receive an extra fee for doing for them what I could not avoid? No, sir, keep your money."

"Well, I declare, if this is not astonishing!" thought Mr. Crisp. "He is out at the elbows, and tar enough on his jacket to paint an anchor. It beats all. But I will not hurt his feelings again." And he withdrew his offer, saying, " So, my young philosopher, I have been one of your serving men, have I ? Well, that is just what I have called myself time and again. But you are the first to take me at my word, and to treat me as the prince treats the lackey that brings the wrong wine. But, since I owe you my life, I can well afford to be your humble servant now. So, what can I do for you ? "

" Well, sir, the boats will soon be laid up for the winter, and I will be out of work. Could you get me a job ashore ? I am not particular, — anything, a chance to teach a school, perhaps."

" But are you equal to that ? "

" I think I am."

" I do not doubt it," said Mr. Crisp, assured by his look of pride. " You will have it, or, what is better, I am in want of a clerk, and if you choose you can come in on your own terms."

" Thank you, thank you, sir. I will do my best to justify your confidence."

" Indeed," said the old merchant, " you talk like an old book-keeper already. Come home with me, and I will see that you are duly settled. But to be frank, Mr. Lawson, he who refuses an honest thousand is not likely to prove particularly sharp. Ah, good evening, sir, there's the dinner-bell. However, I like him," he muttered as the lad withdrew, " and if there is anything in him, he will have a chance to show it. Halloo, Captain Seabreeze (this was the master of the lost ship), do you know that young fellow there just moving off ? "

"Yes, sir, one of my best men, sir; a fine lad, sir, a very fine lad, sir;" and Captain Seabreeze bent before the rich man to whom he was indebted.

"How long has he been with you, Seabreeze?"

"Second season, sir: always on hand; never missed a trip, sir; works like the Devil, sir."

"Captain Seabreeze, I beg you to remember my dislike to profaneness;" and Mr. Crisp turned his back on the unfortunate skipper, who cried out to Malcolm, as soon as he saw him, "I say, lad, look out for number one. The old chap's taken a notion to you, — a notion, sir. Only get religion, and your fortune is made. Oh, he is worth " — and Seabreeze paused till his imagination gathered strength to relieve itself, when he said, "blocks piled upon blocks, and no end to scrip, sir."

"Really, I think I will go home with him."

"Of course, and take my advice. A religious old chap, sir, a very religious old chap, sir; plenty of tracts, sir; take them to heart, — set sail for glory."

"Thank you, Captain, I had quite forgotten that there was such a thing as religion."

"You shan't forget it again, sir. Pitch into the tracts, sir, head foremost. Oyster supper of them, rapid change of heart, sir; Redeemer ready, and tug to golden gate, sir; spirit's steam, sir."

"But why not try it yourself, Captain?"

"Not in me, sir. Tried hard, but could not do it. A born devil, sir, so must go below, sir, must go below;" and exit Captain Seabreeze, an example of profane resignation, while Malcolm went to the grand abode of one of the elect.

Malcolm was overjoyed with his good luck, and went to work with a will to make himself worthy of it. But, alas! to his infinite sorrow, he soon discovered that he was no better adapted to trade now than he had been seven years ago, when he was the employé of the friend, who did not esteem highly "they wild Highland sangs of his," and could not see the fun of a tombstone ride.

He evidently lacked that stern, hard-fisted, indefatigable, though often smiling, shrewdness, or, if you like the term better, the genuine Saxon or Scandinavian aptitude for money-making, which is so common in New Humbleton, and to which so much of its prosperity is owing, as well as so much of its blindness to the beauty of goodness, and this fault in Deacon Crisp's eyes was next to theological infidelity itself. But gratitude influenced the deacon in his favor, and Malcolm continued to stay in his store, notwithstanding the sneering remarks a want of smartness induced his brethren of the quill to make at his expense.

He was discouraged, and, had he not possessed a friend at court, he would have been quite disconsolate, and probably returned to harder, yet perhaps more congenial, labor.

This friend the reader probably suspects, was no other than the fair Jennie herself, the heiress of the palatial residence, and the lumber untold, &c. Not only the romance which attended his introduction to her as the saviour of her father's life, but the gratitude with which he inspired her, told powerfully in his favor. In all other respects, save in social position, he was not unworthy of her, being, all things considered, a young man of pleasing exterior, and the possessor of fine ideas.

From the first hour of her acquaintance with him she had liked him, and as he resided, the honored guest of her father, under the same roof, her liking rapidly ripened into a deeper sentiment.

Malcolm was wiser than she. He realized how foolish it was for him to aspire to the daughter of a millionaire, and did his best to withdraw from the dazzlement.

This conduct of his only increased the love of the fair Jennie, to whom such a proceeding on the part of one of her admirers had all the charm of novelty. Recognizing his superiority to others, and divining that his coldness was only assumed, she could not prevent him from seeing her affection. The young man, almost without being conscious of it, had fallen in love with her. How could he help it? As it were, the gates of a paradise unexpectedly opened unto him, and a fair Eve was there to receive him. He confessed his love.

But the particular parent,—"ay, there's the rub," — what was he to say to this climax? O Brother Crisp, Brother Crisp! what availeth thy Continental Miracle Protection Society in a case of this kind? There is a mouse in thy cupboard.

That venerable personage, when he heard of the above, for he had ears, was wroth, and performed all the antics which the most romantic could demand from a deacon under these circumstances. He stormed and thundered, grew frantic, and, forgetting the Decalogue, swore. In the first fit of his indignation he forgot his indebtedness to the youth, and, yielding to the impulse of the moment, refused to see him again. Then turning to his daughter, who had come with tearful eyes to deprecate his wrath, he would have given her a severe reprimand, had she not, overcome by the intensity of her grief, fainted away. However, as the young lady, notwithstanding the injudicious treatment of the perturbed household, soon revived, his anger returned, and he scolded her well. But the little fairy, who now began to realize her power, was undismayed by his reproaches, and silently persisted in giving Malcolm the first place in her regard. To vanquish the prejudices of her father she now collected her sinking energies, and with all the unconscious art of her sex besieged the heart which Mammon had fortified so strongly. Therefore as days flew by, the deacon had reason to think that he had been a little too precipitate in his dismissal of her lover. His observant child was not slow to perceive her advantage, and, profiting by several favorable opportunities, so represented the facts of the case that he changed his mind, and under certain conditions finally consented to receive Malcolm as his destined son-in-law.

## VI.

### A GOOD IDEA.

THE deacon, having made up his mind to indulge his daughter, wondered what he should do with Malcolm. "Bless me," said he to himself, "what shall I do with the young man? What a pity it is that he has no business capacity! Confound it, I wish I had never brought him here. D—n the rascal (God forgive me the oath)! Fool that I was not to notice it before. I am not only obliged to give him the girl, the pride of my life, but one hundred thousand dollars to keep her alive." Just at this moment, as he pulled out his handkerchief to wipe away the tears the idea of such a sacrifice brought to his eyes, a packet of delicate little tracts fell out upon the floor and fluttered about the room. He stooped to pick them up, and his eye falling upon these words, " Let him be equipped in the armor of the Lord, and sent out to fight the good fight," he muttered in a reflective manner, "Ah! he is not a bad youth after all." Then, remembering how studious he had been, and how attentive to his pious exhortations, he came to the conclusion, as his eye again fell upon the text aforesaid, that he might not make a bad minister, and perhaps an honorable member of the Continental

Miracle Protection Association. So he said, "Upon my word, it is an excellent idea, a divine behest. 'Let us equip him in the armor of the Lord';" and the remainder of the text rolled unctuously forth from his lips. "I will make a minister of him, and as such he will, at least, be quite acceptable to my friends in the faith. To be sure, for a girl in Jennie's position it is a terrible come-down. But God is good, and his ways are not our ways; who knows but that he has sent him to me for some special purpose? The lad is not without character, and his originality is not hostile to the Word. I would not be at all surprised, if he were only subjected to proper influences, he turned out well, and ranked high in the denomination."

Thus it seems that the deacon was not destitute of common sense. He had enough to see, that, notwithstanding the boy's deplorable want of business talent, he was far from being stupid in other respects, and was one of the steadiest of young men; at all events, he was in his opinion good enough for the ministry, as he believed that faithfulness, and not so much great talent, was the prerequisite for that profession. Not only the studiousness and the steadiness of Malcolm pleased him, but he liked him for his regular attendance upon divine service, and for the attention with which he had listened to him when he expounded the "Word" to his own household, which he did a little oftener than was agreeable to it.

The fact was, Malcolm, notwithstanding his originality, was so much occupied attending to his own improvement, that he had but little time to deplore the short-comings of others.  He saw enough in the Calvinistic system of religion to attract his respect, if not to awaken enthusiasm for it.  His studies and duties, as a laborer in the vineyard of man, so absorbed him that he was gradually losing the exacting God of his childhood.  In this respect, however, like all healthy minds, he was making that transition of Being which has been compared to the molting process, without the gnawing self-consciousness so often accompanying it.  Yet he was still under the influence of that kind of superstition which, although often found in Christian churches, is free from bigotry or fear.  His vision had not yet reached the traditionary errors which impede the progress of true religion, and hinder the free exercise of Reason among the people.  Therefore, since he found a certain nourishment in the pastures of Presbyterianism, it was as natural for him to read the Bible and attend church as to wear a fashionable hat and take it off to the family minister.  It had not yet occurred to him that he was only a Christian, and that if he intended to devote himself to the improvement of his race, it might be necessary to become a Liberal.

In regard to his present creed, he puts us in mind of a child still so charmed with its musical toy, that it remains without curiosity as to the source of the pleasant sounds.  But the period of inquiry had yet to come, and the creed be sacrificed.  Yet what of that?  Men must put away childish things, even the nursery literature which once afforded them, or still may supply, food for wonderment. It is strange that the madness of which Don Quixote is the well-known type, should repeat itself with such regularity from generation to generation. In vain we refute, burn, annihilate the legends which give rise to it. The consequences of the perusal remain, and, blending with the inherent weaknesses of humanity, excite the astonishment, ridicule, or terror of ordinary minds. Behold the Knights of the Hour, each bearing on his banner (newspaper) the *ism* of his adoration, the badge of his order, and the emblem of his cause; each attacking the other, or vainly struggling against the wind mills of modern thought, or galloping full tilt, with unexpected velocity, upon flocks of inoffensive sheep.

Poor Malcolm read his Revelations, and, like nearly all young men of the present day, was not sure whether he believed them or not. In his individual capacity, he had to yet undergo the Protestant Reformation, but perhaps without the experience of much benefit.

"I say, sir," asked a smart boy in a bookseller's store, "have ye got any books for boys that haven't got any religion in them?"

# VII.

WHAT JENNIE SAID TO IT, NAMELY, THE GOOD IDEA, AND HOW MALCOLM GOT THE BENEFIT OF IT AND WAS DULY INSTALLED AS THE FAVORED INDIVIDUAL.

JENNIE was delighted with this opportune conclusion of her parent, namely, to equip her lover in the armor of the Lord, and send him out to fight the good fight with — whatever you please to add, dearly beloved readers. After a fitting expression of her gratitude and joy, she said that she had always liked ministers, particularly those of the new school; and Malcolm, with his fine mind and spiritual expression, would make a good one. Then she said, "And he will have a splendid field for the exercise of his talents. How good of you, dear, dear papa, to think of this! An angel from Heaven must have inspired you." And she sang, "Happy day, happy day," but in so indecorus a tone that the deacon rebuked her, and told her that, if she intended to marry a minister, she must become more sedate in her manners. She straightway vowed repentance, and flew up stairs on the wings of excitement, to write and tell Malcolm all about it.

Malcolm, meanwhile, had been in a troubled state

of mind.  He felt keenly the outrageous conduct of the deacon.

As soon as he left the house he returned to the office, where he wrote to both father and daughter, thanking the former for his past kindness, and bidding the other an affectionate farewell till the advent of a brighter day.  He then went home to new lodgings in a still more melancholy mood.  This expulsion from his recent Eden, and from the presence of his Eve, was worse than the one he had already experienced in childhood.  He was disconsolate, and for a time was unable to do anything but dwell upon the adverse occurrence.  At last he began to raise his drooping head, and look about him, as his purse, in unconscious sympathy with his misfortune, had gone into a decline.  He tried the lakes again, and found the best cure for his unhappiness in hard work.

On his return from his first trip he found a letter waiting for him, asking him to call at Mr. Crisp's office, as that gentleman had something important to communicate.

He went.  Mr. Crisp, who was amiability itself, received him in the kindest manner.  "My dear boy," he began, looking up from his cash-book, and sticking his pen behind his ear, "I confess I was a little hasty.  For the moment the Evil One got the upper hand of me, and I treated you badly.  But (here he looked resolute) I shall make amends.  You will forget it when I inform you of what I, with

God's help intend to do for you.  To be candid, I was disappointed that Jennie should fix her choice upon you, for I had other views for her.  Young Fitzmouse, of Grasp, Fitsmouse, Catch, & Co., had proposed for her, and being the son of a dear friend and personally very eligible, I had made up my mind in his favor.  But it seems that Providence has interposed, and I will not rebel against his will, or, indeed, against my own good sense; for, after all, your character is of the best; and I remember now what I am sorry to have forgotten once, namely, that I owe you my life."

"Oh, Mr. Crisp, do not remind me of that."

"You are generous, Malcolm, and I am constrained to be even with you.  The barriers of conventionalism shall tumble, and you shall have my child, and in due time all that I possess."  And the deacon leaned back in his chair, and looked up to see the effect of his eloquence.

Malcolm was speechless for a moment, and then, rising, he took Mr. Crisp's hand, and said, "You bewilder me, sir.  Your kindness fills me so that I feel as if I could move heaven and earth to repay it."

"Gently, gently, my son," and the deacon smiled.  "I am less ambitious than you, and do not look for so vast a show of gratitude.  All that I wish in return is a docile mind and a willing heart, and if you could only take my advice, and be a little more of a business man, I would be quite satisfied.  But since that is out of the question, it has occurred to me that you might make an excellent preacher.  What do you say to the ministry for a profession?

"The ministry!" and the young man was speechless again.

"Yes, sir, the ministry," was the pompous reply, and the deacon withdrew a thumb from the arm-hole of his vest, and lifted the other from its interrogative position on the desk, evidently requiring the help of both hands for the speech he was about to make,— "the service of man for the sake of God ; and if you will but dwell for a moment upon all that he has done for us, it will sharpen your intelligence. Infinite Self-sacrifice demands entire unselfishness on our part; and is there not endless labor before those who rejoice in the gift of Revelation? And if the chief end of man is to glorify God, and enjoy him forever, it is time for him to be up and doing. Thus, Malcolm, I open the door of a great future, and it remains with you, now, whether you will buckle on the armor of righteousness. I need hardly say that what with radicals, spiritists, and all manner of infidels, the world is in a pretty bad way; hence great need of faithful officers."

"This is a surprise, Mr. Crisp. But I appreciate the idea. My great concern is that I am not worthy of a commission in your army. Heretofore, I have been only a private, and hardly know the word of command. Of course I can learn, but I haven't even thought of spiritual strategy."

"Malcolm, this is not a subject for levity," and the deacon colored.

"Pardon me, sir. I did not mean to speak lightly or disrespectfully. But I am not pious enough to carry Heavenly Messages and take orders that I cannot faithfully fulfill; Dr. Pluffle says I talk like a heathen, and it may be true. Nor can I tell what ails me; but in regard to theology I feel wofully numb. However, accept my thanks for the interest you take in me."

"Well, Malcolm, I declare you are the most singular person I ever saw! What is there in this wide world of ours to hinder you from accepting the Revealed Word, and devoting yourself to the redemption of Humanity?"

"I do not know, unless it is unfitness for the task. I see that it is no small affair; yet I gladly entertain the project; and, indeed, as I see into the future, it appears more feasible. Captain Seabreeze said that I was a born preacher, and urged me to get religion by all means."

"I did not know," said the deacon, sharply, "that he was particularly religious."

"Not he! But he is fully alive to the advantages of the Faith, even while he deplores his innate deviltry."

"To save my life, boy, I cannot tell whether your simplicity is real or feigned. But I must think that you, who come of sound Presbyterian stock, would gladly enter upon the noblest vocation of all. There is not a young Christian in the country who would not go into ecstasies at an offer like this."

"Do not misunderstand me, sir. You know that it is my habit to speak just as I feel; and it hurts me not to. The prospect you unfold is dazzling, and my only misgiving is that I am not equal to the task. It is true that I have always revered genuine Christians, but I never liked to call myself one, lest I should not be quite up to the mark. Still, since your desire concurs with my ambition, I will go to college and exert myself to learn the Truth."

"That's the proper spirit, my son; that's the proper spirit. You see the propriety of adopting some profession; and what more congenial to the soul than the acquisition of Truth?"

Here the deacon was interrupted by the unexpected entrance of Miss Crisp, who ran to meet her lover; and, taking him by both hands, she said, —

"O, Malcolm! you are come back at last, and I am so glad! And this splendid plan of papa's! You are to be a minister, — just think, — my minister! And we will all be so happy again. Come home with me now, do; I have so much to tell you." And thus urgent, quite careless of appearances and the gaze of envious clerks, the young princess led Malcolm out of her father's private office, through the palatial store into the buzzing street ("that centipede in harness," as Mr. Sweep has it).

The deacon glanced after them with a deep sigh, but in a moment he smiled again, for had he not — even while he put an indifferent Calvinist in a fair way to obtain a more living faith, and thus vindicate his Lord — manifested enthusiasm in the service of his Maker, and, at the same time, got rid of a serious domestic botheration?

Deacon Crisp was a rare compound of amiability, shrewdness, genuine piety, rapacity, and superstition, and, as in all men, with few exceptions, it depended on circumstances whether vice or virtue had the upper hand. Malcolm and he were related, else they would not have met. But small as Mr. Crisp is, faithful adherence to the Letter makes him large enough to contain the world, — a tight fit truly, and the reader will allow for the straining.

"An exact spiritual balance, and the just regulation of events," says Prof. Knitting Needle, "are maintained by obedience to two laws: the law of objective self-preservation, which enjoins strict attention to business and to the practical in general; and the law of subjective integrity, which enjoins devotion to the ideal, and *reasonable* self-sacrifice for the same. According to the first law, Jesus, Socrates, and countless martyrs fell, — and legitimately so, all things considered; for their ideas, consistently put in practice, would have resulted in the destruction of the letter of the law, and, consequently, of the means of government, to the deterioration of the body politic. Whereas, had the martyrs reasonably conformed to the existing prejudices and established institutions, and thus given the objective its due weight, a proper balance might have been instituted to the realization of happiness for all."

But Malcolm didn't know this, and he could not but think it strange that, instead of giving up all for Jesus' sake, he was forced to take all and follow him. Even the best of circumstances will conspire against one. The deacon gave Malcolm to understand that he desired a sound Christian to marry his daughter,

## VIII.

### A BLACK SPOT.

SUCH, then, were the circumstances that led to the engagement of the young people whom we have already described in conversation with one another in the luxurious parlor of the deacon. Society, when informed of it, being as oracular as ever, stared in amazement, and said, "Who would have thought it? What an infatuation! Both father and daughter are mad." But Mr. Crisp was fond of having his own way, and Malcolm and Jennie were too much in love to care what was said about them.

It is not necessary for us to describe all that passed in the magnificent domicile, and the good city of Bragville up to the day of Malcolm's departure for the Orient to join the academy of divinity there. The fortnight that preceded it was one prolonged dream of delight, — and how could it be otherwise? Both were in the Eden of first love, as we have already intimated. The youth saw the ideal for which he had toiled and striven upon the eve of realization, and the maiden was happy in the possession of a lover, who not only answered her romantic tastes, but loved her for the good that was in her.

But there was just one black spot on their present horizon, and they felt its presence, although they could not be said to see it.

The Rev. Jehosaphat Pluffle, D.D., was the favored pastor and the trusted friend of Mr. Crisp, and the treasurer of the Continental Miracle Protection Association. As this gentleman was still single, he had for some time past been looking upon Miss Jane with admiring eyes, but, as she had never given him a word of encouragement, he had studiously withheld from her ear the avowal of the flame that consumed him. He had hoped that she might experience a "change of heart," and therefore had not felt disappointed until "that young Darklyn vagabond," as he was pleased to term her lover, came along and knocked his hopes on the head. Then he really did feel the need of all his faith to bear him up in his troubles, and, thanks either to that or a good constitution, slowly recovered. His hopes revived as, looking over the domain of the future, he thought he saw some chances in his favor.

Jehosaphat Pluffle was neither more nor less than an ordinary hypocrite. He was one of those big, pluffy, shambling dignitaries of the Church, with a lisp, who are as strong in the faith and the spirit as they are weak in the flesh and principle. But what did mere lack of physical beauty matter to one of his faith and denomination, to one of his social position and excessive unctuosity? Evidently speaking from his past experience, he said to himself, as he compared himself to the fair Jennie, "I shall do my best to extinguish her carnal vision. I shall so illuminate my humble person with the magic name of the Lord that I shall be as one transfigured in her sight. Verily, the name availeth much with the father already. I cannot but believe that I am acceptable to him. Who knows what may happen to the young fellow? I doubt much if he be a worthy vessel to hold the holy oil. I shall rely upon the Lord, and bide my time."

Therefore Jehosaphat bided his time, and in the interim neglected no opportunity of disparaging the youth to his destined father-in-law. "My good brother in the Lord," he said to him, shortly after he heard of the engagement, "I fear you have been a little hasty in this matter. Have you thoroughly satisfied yourself about the antecedents of Lawson? You would invest him in the sacred cloth, and make an evangelist of him! You certainly do fill me with surprise."

"Why not?" said the deacon. "I know him to be a most exemplary lad. He saved my life, as you well know; and there is Jennie, who loves him to distraction. He is sure to excel in the ministry. I never saw anything out of the way in the boy, save perhaps a little willful humor. It never occurred to me to concern myself about his antecedents."

"The Evil One," lisped Dr. Pluffle, with increased unction of manner, "is very deceitful; the best of us are often taken by surprise. I regret to say — and, verily, were I not moved by the spirit to say what I now say, I should be silent — that your protégé hath appeared to me to be a little bit wayward. Remember, were I not your trusty friend, and had I not your welfare at heart, I should not take the liberty of mentioning this to you. You will hardly believe me when I tell you that when I exhorted Mr. Lawson to stand up with the rest of the flock for the Lord, he only smiled in reply,—yes, Brother Crisp, in reply to my earnest exhortations he smiled vainly and most unbecomingly. His affections may not be so firmly placed on things above as we both might desire." Here the right reverend gentleman paused, and his vision rolled serenely down the black silk covered slope of his bosom, as if his affections were located to his perfect satisfaction.

"I don't know about that," said the deacon, who had more common sense than Dr. Pluffle. "I thought the boy was religious enough. I am sorry you don't like him. But he'll improve. Oratone Buzz, Progressive Bungle, and Hezekiah Graves will bring him out all right. I see nothing to hinder him from becoming one of our foremost miracle protectors."

"It grieveth me to the heart, my good brother, to dampen thy enthusiasm; but that smile, brother, that smile. It haunts my memory and will not away. Verily, there is much in his favor," here he could not suppress a groan; "I do trust he shall prove worthy of thee and thine. Good morning, brother, I must leave thee here;" and, shaking hands, the gentlemen parted, the one to condole with a sick parishioner who was about to die in the Lord, and the other to return to his cash-book.

But did the reverend Pluffle have any ground at all for his aspiration to the hand of Miss Crisp? None: excepted the simple fact that she was superstitious enough to regard clergymen as sacred beings, who were much more intimately connected with Divinity than ordinary mortals. The girl really believed that she had a soul, and was quite willing to do all she could for it consistently with her ordinary mode of life and with her fondness for a good time. Therefore she listened with at least a semblance of patience to the stream of pious words which Pluffle poured into her ears when he called to attend to her spiritual wants, or seek the transfiguration of himself in her sight.

As Dr. Pluffle was in the habit of calling himself a miserable sinner, we simply take the liberty to represent him as such. The reader will sympathize with our readiness to take him at his word.

"Confound the obstinacy of her carnal vision," growled Pluffle in an undertone, as that quality of the young lady would wander from the contemplation of her pastor to the prospect of her alliance with the young Darklyn student, and dwelt upon the entertainments with which she intended to inaugurate the happy event.

"Do you like parties, Dr. Pluffle?" she asked once, interrupting him in one of his peculiar refrains.

"To what kind of parties do you refer, my dear child? If you refer to the conventicles of Fashion, I should say, 'No,' although it is necessary that I should attend them sometimes and warn the fold, that is, in a friendly manner, you know, against indulgence in perishable pleasures, and remind them of the duties they owe to the Lamb. A serious moment in the midst of gaiety does not come amiss. But the parties in which I take pleasure are the blissful communions and conferences of the saints. How glad I would be, nay, how glad the Lord would be, and what rejoicing there would be round the throne, if you, sweet sister, would give up your heart to the benign influences of the Spirit, and be wholly one of us."

The young lady shuddered at this display of feeling on the part of the Knight of the Woeful Figure; for it occurred to her that if she were going to be the wife of a minister, she would have to participate in the communion of saints, and in all sorts of sepulchral things. Her only comfort was the thought that Malcolm was too lively ever to become so spiritually dingy as Dr. Pluffle. However, feeling that she must, as a minister's wife, become a little more serious in her deportment, she could not but be a little conscience-stricken at the thought of her spiritual deficiencies.

"I fear," she replied confidingly, "that I am awfully wicked, Dr. Pluffle. I am so fond of my kind of parties that I have not been to a prayer-meeting for a month."

"Alas!" lisped Dr. Pluffle, turning up the whites of his eyes, and sighing with concentrated piety, "we are all very wicked, and were it not for the Blood where would we be?" The last part of this sentence came out with a barely perceptible jerk, and, after darting a glance at Miss Crisp, the eyes resumed their meek expression, and again shone with calm resignation.

"You certainly ought to bethink yourself in this matter, my dear sister. Much dependeth upon the active participation of the wife in the evangelical duties of her husband. I would gladly assist you in your search for grace, see, in fact, attend personally to your growth therein, that you might fairly flourish in the Lord, and bring forth good fruit;" and he smiled a benign smile.

"Thank you, Dr. Pluffle: how good of you to take this interest in me. I will accept your guidance, and hope I shall not prove an unworthy sheep. But excuse me now." She had heard her lover's ring, and was now hearing him ascend the stairs towards the library; and, scarcely waiting for a reply, she courtesied to Dr. Pluffle and hastily withdrew.

Jehosaphat also heard the ring, and, knowing well who came, he gnashed his teeth as, with forced composure, he turned to a stereoscope and appeared to be intent upon its wonders.

# IX.

## FACING ALL WAYS, OR THE KNIGHT OF THE RAINBOW CREED, NUMBER ONE, OF ORIENTAL FAME.

WE were about to write a long dissertation upon preaching, when we happened, just as we laid the life of the Apostle Paul on the table, to cast our eye on one of the printed oracles of that goddess of world-wide notoriety known as Madam Demorest, which so well expressed the true character of that function of some Christian ministers, that we think it a sin to leave it without due recognition. Listen, then, O votaries of all divinities both secular and religious to the oracles. We only change a word or two, to make the sense more complete and the style more attractive.

"'*Truth* unadorned is adorned the most,'" a paradox, now obsolete, the worth and truth of which was undoubtedly accepted in those good old days when nine *sheets*, of ordinary *size*, made an *ad*-dress for the most *particular* of our maternal ancestors, with a remnant left for 'fixing over.'

"The *clergymen* of the nineteenth century believe that a *florid style* and *other rhetorical* ornaments, though not indispensable, are important items in one's *sermons*, and when appropriately selected (always remembering that quality and not quantity is the indication of a refined taste), they certainly add to the grace and beauty of the appearance, be the *subject* either a fair or a plain one. Just as a picture beautiful and valuable on the bare canvas when placed in the surrounding of a chaste and beautiful frame, so these dainty *rhetorical* ornaments, in all their exquisite designs, bring to the sight and mind of the observer a sense of peculiar fitness when tastefully *preached* by fair *clergymen.*" *

O mighty spirit of Jesus of Nazareth! why art thou not here to see the adornment of thy once simple Truth? What has become of the humility with which thou didst inaugurate the crusade against Hypocrisy? Wouldst thou recognize it in the rainbow hues of the current theology wherewith it must be attired ere it can become acceptable to us? Tell us, prithee, whether the present fashion be a token of the fullness of the soul, the flowering of our prosperity, or, like the rank growth of a corpse's hair, the product of decay.

It is plain that the girls of the period are as divine as the ministers. By contriving to alter a word now and then we could turn the fashion books into religious magazines. Please substitute to correspond the following words: "Beauty," "corpulent," "ladies," "jewelry," "face," "worn," "ladies." It is not hard to see where they belong. The empire of clothes is still paramount; that of the soul is barely begun. Fashion is a Pharaoh, and his heart grows daily harder.

After those sublimities of Fashion it is hardly worth our while to tell you about Oratone. But as we have a story to relate we must describe his rev-

---

\* Madam Demorest's Bulletin of Ladies' and Children's Fashions, Fall and Winter, '72-'73. The chapter on Jewelry, p. 57.

erence to the best of our ability. As this fair clergyman represents a certain class of orators, we think it a duty to draw attention to the good and the ill that is in him. He was stout, fat, handsome, and *not* yet fifty years old. Quite frank and open in his manners, and characterized by a carriage in which pomposity and jauntiness struggled for the mastery, his whole appearance betokened an impulsively generous but exceedingly vain man. Having then, as we intimate, many physical advantages, these were admirably displayed by his peculiar style of dress, which had just enough of the clerical to satisfy the deacons, who believe in keeping up a prayerful appearance, and just enough of the poetic to make him interesting to the fair sex. Being very good natured and extremely affable, he was the favorite of every one, especially of the young girls, who thought him "perfectly splendid." And he really was. How well he looked as he stepped up the pulpit stairs in his peculiar style of mingled stateliness and genial foppishness, and threw himself into the sacred chair, covering his brow with one hand, as if penetrated by a fitting sense of the solemnity of the moment! In a charming manner he would come to himself again, and while one delicate, fat hand would fall negligently by his side, his head would be thrown up with a nonchalant air; and the lustrous locks which had slightly overhung his vision being thrown aside with a skillful toss of the head, he would treat the congregation to a most benignant stare.

But when the Rev. Oratone arose and prayed, the

sunlight through an opportune crack in the shade of the window parallel with the pulpit descending upon his beautiful head, and crowning it with a halo such as those we are wont to find painted around the head of the Lord, in the favorite pictures of him, what a worshipful sight! And his splendid voice, how it gradually increased from a faint, inarticulate murmur, like the cooing of doves, into a deep, melodious sound, and, swelling, broke upon the ear like the music of the surf on a sandy shore! How tuneful it could be, and yet, when the occasion required it, loud and menacing as thunder among the mountains!

It was really a treat to see him rise and hear him preach from his favorite text. When the melody of the hymn had gradually subsided, he would arise with a very imposing mien, as if he were about to propound a most unheard-of truth, and, looking first to the left with an authoritative glance, say impressively, "I seek not mine own glory," getting nothing but a wink from the fortunate occupants of the front pews in reply, who, being fully impressed with this revelation, he would turn to the right and repeat it with a similar result; which momentous labor being successfully performed, he would take his audience fairly and squarely in the centre, and again the words, "I seek not mine own glory," would be poured unctuously forth. Then Madam Demorest's idea would be carried out to the letter, and the appearance completed with *éclat*.

Yes, indeed: Oratone was a most remarkable man and did a great deal of good, but only with his voice, his enemies cruelly remarked; for with brains he was not particularly blessed. Whether he were really gifted in the latter respect or not, no one could truly affirm. At all events, he made a much better show than most of his brethren in words. His tact was admirable, illimitable, and with the magic thereof he could raise thousands for the hundreds they produced, and invariably preached to a full house, while they were compelled to put up with four walls, six people, and the sexton for an auditory. He belonged to the great Independent Spirit Navigation Denomination, being vice-admiral at least of that astounding organization in Christ.

When Malcolm first heard this dignitary preach, which he did as soon as he came to Huberton University, he hardly knew what to make of the phenomenon, his early Presbyterianism not having prepared him for anything of the kind. However, he too experienced the fascination of his "taking style," and could not avoid loving the man, being quite able to sympathize with a companion who said that, if he belonged to the other sex, he might resign his heart as well as his soul into his keeping. The competition for the hand of his reverence had been great. We cannot enumerate all the gifts which had been showered on his devoted head, but this every one knows for a fact, — namely, he sent a cart-load of elegant slippers, gaily embroidered in gold and wool, to the Home of the Superannuated. Who gave them to him? Do not blush, fair daughters of Columbia; nobody blames you, bless your pious little hearts. It is for that mysterious conclave popularly known as the Standing Committee for whom we reserve our admonitions, and whose attention we would earnestly call to the latest cases of ecclesiastical iniquity on record. Listen and tremble, O venerable defenders of the Faith! If you enshrine a good-looking fellow in the highest seat of a splendid edifice, and get him to speak as one having authority from Above on the themes most dear to the heart of both woman and man, while the most sensuous music adds to the glory of his presence and of his eloquence, you must not be astonished that the belles of the congregation should suddenly evince a marked concern about their souls and prefer the society of the shepherd to that of such sheep as yourselves.

## X.

## THE RAINBOW CREED.

THE Rainbow Creed! The Rainbow Creed! O reader, wouldn't you like a clear definition thereof? Of course. But we are not going to knock the universe into a cocked hat for your particular benefit. So we leave that splendid phenomenon among the mysteries of the skies, and trust to your ingenuity to discover what we mean. What can you expect from so enlightened a doctor as O. Buzz but a belief worthy of his beautiful voice? For, excepting his hatred of heresy, and a little worldliness, incidental, of course, to those who are not remarkable for self-esteem (considering sundry articles of their creed), we have no more against him than we have against ourselves. For, being satirical, we cannot forget that we, unfortunately, are among the goats who cannot share with the Lord's sheep the splendors of Heaven. And so disagreeable is this thought that our only consolation is, that since God became human for sinners' sake, we are willing to be anything for the sake of reclaiming the depraved.

Yes, Oratone was a great favorite, and, tell you the truth, it is with great pleasure we condescend to portray his belief in its true colors.

The conservative liked him because he showed sufficient respect for their Peters, Pauls, Tabernacles, and what not. The semi-conservative or half-radical liked him because he mentioned science with a certain amount of respect, and took the trouble to try and reconcile it with Genesis and Exodus; and the ultra-liberal liked him as everybody did, simply because he was such an off-hand, free-and-easy good fellow, who cracked some of the best jokes going, and never was severe on anybody except the Devil and Andrew Johnson. But J. Sweep understands him better than we.

"Did it ever occur to thee, O Reader, to think what Oratone Buzz and his friends could do for the religious life of the country, — for the religious life of the country? I went to hear him and Dr Lullaby preach, as advertised, expecting to find, from the high tone of the announcement, a couple of Isaiahs who would go for the iniquity of the times like the Pittsburg thunder-storm; but found only, to my permanent surprise, sundry sleek, "cultivated" gentlemen, who stood up for their denominational interests in the pleasantest style conceivable. But the speeches were taking, and the prayers superb. What more is needed in this age of religious independence, when the Sun of Godliness shines so as to create on the surface of the falling sinners such amiable images of himself? But how dreadful the thought of assimilation with the beams! Alas, poor Buzz! what a deprivation to think thy honored self-existence should be swallowed up in God according to the dismal forebodings of the Pantheists! Permit me, O most potent knight of the rainbow, to relieve thy mind. There is not the smallest danger of it. Buzz thou wast born, and Buzz thou shalt die. 'Tis true, in the sunshine of God thou baskest now, like the glittering insect with the sting in its tail, and, taking to thyself airs thereat, thou buzzest in His face, even while thou, by thine own confession, art the worm's inferior. Know for good that the Son of Man is God, and that thou indeed art nothing, simply because thou art Buzz, and for no other reason under the sun."—*J. Sweep's Autobiography.*

# XI.

## A MOST INCOMPREHENSIBLE THING.

THE time at length arrived for the young people to separate. It was a bitter hour for both, but Hope and Faith were there to illuminate the future, and promise a speedy reunion. They parted exchanging vows of constancy and other expressions of regard. Malcolm was soon himself again. With such a Dulcinea as the fair Jennie, who would not be glad to equip himself in the sacred armor, and go out to fight the good fight, wind-mills or no wind-mills!

Malcolm soon arrived in Huberton, the city of his destination, and, presenting his letters of introduction to the faculty of the college, was graciously received ; and, thanks to the influence of his patron, the celebrated miracle protector, Mr. Crisp, the janitor appointed him to one of the best rooms in the building.

In a short time he felt quite at home, and gave himself up to his studies with most untiring zeal. He was indefatigable. Entirely absorbed by his beloved books, he rarely slept more than five hours, and scarcely ever went out to spend an evening at the theatre, or as the guest of some hospitable family. Had he not possessed a constitution of iron, he would have succumbed to the pressure on his brain. He was cautioned against immoderation in this respect. But, like one who has commenced to run down a steep hill, he could not stop himself. The boy realized his ignorance, as Bunyan's Pilgrim did the burden upon his shoulders, and he hurried to get rid of it without the incessant groaning that characterized Christian on his way to relief.

As yet there was only one thing to trouble him, and that was the prayer question. Heretofore the Lord's Prayer had been ample for him and his little wants, but now it was different. The Hubertonians, judging from the salaries they paid the gifted in the art of supplication, were particularly fond of long prayers, and if he intended to make himself an acceptable knight, it was quite necessary to cultivate a prayerful spirit. Yet there were a few difficulties in the way of his attempt to acquire proficiency in this branch of the service. His early piety had already taught him that prayer should be the free, spontaneous request for whatever one desired at the hand of God. But intuitively or experimentally being aware that that Being has a pardonable fondness for helping those who are wise enough to help themselves, he could not see that he gained anything by the mere utterance of his wishes. He was, on the other hand, strongly inclined to look upon public prayer as a vain display, and a mere evaporation of energy that might be more profitably employed. And the more he studied, the more lively this antipathy of his against it became, so that, as the days flew by, he grew almost ashamed of asking God to increase the wealth of his universe by improving either himself or others. "How can people," he observed to a friend, "expect supernatural aid, when they will not take the trouble to fulfill the natural conditions of health and improvement. On all sides I see individuals, not remarkable for love of goodness, asking favors of God, as if he were not already there to second every honest effort towards improvement. Considering, then, the Infinite Power of self-help already possessed by the world, it is a mystery to me that it should always be asking for more. And I suppose this is why I exhibit so little fluency in addressing the Heavens, and also why I should prefer Endeavor — sweet, honest Endeavor — to that which is ordinarily termed 'prayer.' The former certainly has been the food of my life, and in regard to the latter, if it can be called the bread of life, it tastes strongly of something spurious. For, to be sincere with you, although I sometimes lead in prayer, I often feel that I am doing wrong. However, I appease my conscience with the thought that true prayer is simply a kind of poetry natural to those who love and reverence the Creator. And I am only sorry that I should make so poor a figure in trying to do at stated times what ought to be the spontaneous outpouring of my spirit. But this unpleasant experience of mine may be due to a perversity of disposition which will, I hope, wear away, according as my heart opens to the Spirit of God."

"If that view of prayer be correct," said his friend, "how can we find words sufficiently expressive of our regard for those gifted beings who can, at a moment's warning, rise and pour forth a stream of poetry sufficient to float and carry away a whole fleet of humble vessels."

The following incident in the life of the late Dr. McLeod, of Glasgow in Scotland, he read with great edification. That gentleman, in company with Dr. Watson, another clergyman, was crossing a lake in the Highlands in a small boat. McLeod was a very large man and Watson a small one. They were surprised in the middle of the lake by a terrific squall. The rest of the passengers, consisting of sundry old women, being dreadfully frightened, implored the doctors to pray. Both lifted up their faces and were about to comply with the request, when a stalwart boatman turned round and said, " Stop there, 'minsturs,' the wee ane can pray as lang as he likes, but the big ane must tak' an oar."

Said Malcolm in one of his best moments: " I am here to learn the Truth ; and to this end, were it not for false desires, I could count my years as pennies, and fling them one by one into the hand of Death to pay my way. Why must I stop to speak like the rest ? Surely that cannot be prayer which hinders me so ; and if it is prayer how strange it is that I cannot pray unless I imitate somebody."

What first drew Malcolm's attention to this subject was rather an amusing incident in his scholastic experience. For a few days another student had shared his room, and when night arrived both went to bed and arose in the morning in entire oblivion of the necessity of prayer. At last Brown, as the other student was called, a dapper, little, red-headed fellow, came to Malcolm and said in a very solemn tone, "It seems to me that we have not been faithful to our Eternal interests; but, not to speak of these, if we intend to be Christian ministers it is very necessary that we should give some time to prayer. Ought we not to exercise ourselves in private, that we may excel in the public performance of the devotional function.?"

"Certainly, friend," exclaimed Malcolm, who at the time actually felt the force of his chum's remark, "ease of utterance is essential."

"Well," said Brown, in genuine sacerdotal style, "I'll officiate to-night and you will in the morning."

"All right," said Malcolm, who had again resumed his pen.

That night Brown knelt, and, after making an excellent prayer, rose and "turned in" in an excellent humor with himself. Malcolm envied him his flow of words, and asked how he contrived to pray so easily. That embryo public instructor called to him, from under the blankets, that faith was the key to the door of that gift, and that he ought to give it as much attention as he could.

Next morning Malcolm arose as usual, entirely forgetting the promised officiation. Not so his friend, who piously informed him that it was "his turn." Thereupon they both knelt, in "the trailing garments of the night," each at his own bedside, and Malcolm lifted up his voice. He had hardly reached the end of the first sentence, when a most overpowering sense of the absurdity of the whole proceeding came over him, so that he could not utter a word. He broke down most infamously, to the amazement of little Brown, who, removing a sanctimonious finger from his left eye, looked round to see what was keeping him. Poor Malcolm, who naturally wondered how Brown was taking this stoppage in the transmission of the message to the gods, also removed a finger from the eye nearest the expectant hearer, and turned his head slightly in his direction. Their eyes met, and for a moment gazed into one another, the one indicating profound amazement, and the other a vague anxiety. What were they to do? Suddenly the ludicrousness of the situation told on Malcolm so powerfully that he could not repress the mirth that bubbled to his lips. Brown caught the infection, and, affected likewise, the gentle mirth rapidly grew into peals of convulsive merriment. It is needless to say that from that day to this these young men never officiated for each other.

But Malcolm, notwithstanding all this budding of his naturally radical mind, was still under some superstitious influences. He blamed his unemotional nature for his repugnance to prayer by word of mouth. His words were, "I am not in step with the rest of the troops. I must get in as soon as I can, or cease to march in the ranks." He made no secret of this remarkable deficiency, and it was soon entered in the books of the Faculty against him. His destined father-in-law was informed of it, and he was suddenly treated to an affectionate but Christian letter, in which Mr. Crisp sharply told him that if he wished to retain his friendship, he must not reject the sweet spirit of prayer. Poor Malcolm! this preference of his for the tough spirit of noiseless effort was most unfortunate.

Beyond this defect, there was as yet nothing to mar his reputation for "soundness," beyond a little carelessness in the display of his humor. But since Malcolm's early experience of prayer is not, perhaps, deep enough to give the full significance thereof, we call upon Mr. Sweep to append a word to this chapter.

"Who dares," says he, with that defiant air of omniscience he loves to assume, "to say aught against the common custom of ages, where, like grass-roots in the soil, the sons of men meet and intermingle? The deepest thoughts, noblest acts, have started, like mailed Minervas from the brains of gods, under the influence of prayer. But what sort of prayer was it? O my brother, mistake not the peacock voice of vanity and the groans of indolent sin for the noise of the many tides of energy as they rise to sweep all obstacles from their path, as in the case of such ministers as Oliver Cromwell and John Bunyan. Think again, Mr. Twenty Minutes Long, ere you roll your soul into the empty O's, the naughts of naughtiness which bubble from your lips. Some prayers are the shouts of the Faith which moves the mountains, and rides, like Apollo, in a chariot of fire, the pith of the universe."

## XII.

### A GLANCE AT THE TIMES.

HOW happens it that prophecy has vanished from the earth? Artifice is ever the death of true greatness. "I see," says J. Sweep, "man must return to the natural state of the Spirit." In the days of savage innocence and poetic knowledge, in spite of the absence of science — how superior the method of reform! The ancient reformer did not get up a speech that would take, but got up himself; and God got up with him, and girding their loins, the great religions of the world flowed from their hearts. How is it that we, with all our literature and science, are obliged to gyrate round their accidental words? No wonder the sons of Atlas, the laborers who bear the burden of the world, seeing how well they can dispense with the guidance of the Church, maintain they can do without any kind of government. Strange sounds, indeed, are heard in the silence of the night, and still stranger shapes hover in the opacity overhead, threatening at any moment to take new forms of destruction. The time, it seems to us, has arrived for all people to speak just as they think, regardless of the infirmities of their dispositions, which, in spite of the most profound artifice, are clear to the eye of the seer.

# XIII.

## THE VALLEY OF THE SHADOW.

THERE is a fatal blindness in civilization. Tacitus, the Roman prophet, critic and gentleman, with all his advantages, could see nothing but a baneful superstition in the rising faith of his day, Christianity.

A new superstition has appeared in our midst, and certainly, as far as our vision goes, with greater circumstances of success than were originally possessed by Christianity, excepted, however, the rather startling fact that no Jesus has yet died for it. Nor can it ever be hoped by its most distinguished supporters that any person will be led to do so until he has ascertained that the eternity of the soul is not a Debatable Land. In view, then, of the monstrosities of modern religion we do not know whether to laugh or weep at the phenomenology of the Spirit, whether interpreted by a Hegel or the latest reporter of the last theological newspaper. But since we realize the necessity of doing something, we cut the knot of our dilemma by doing both as faithfully as we can, not forgetting our own entanglement in the net of involuntary Fate.

The magnitude of knowledge current concerning the religions of all nations bewildered Malcolm, but why the first principles of any one in particular were not better appreciated and applied, puzzled him beyond the power of language to express. And it was this experience which first led him to believe that he had as good a right to think as he pleased as either Jew or Gentile, Christian or Mohammedan. Thus armed and equipped by this opportune solution of his difficulties, he had no conscientious scruples whatever in rejecting the mixed philosophy and dogmatic assertion of his teachers for the natural religion of his own heart, which told him that he, too, insignificant as he felt himself to be in his relations to mankind, could aspire to a direct revelation from God. And, unconsciously inspired by this thought, he applied himself to the study of whatever was likely to throw light on the mystery of his being. But, of course the reader will see that this idea in its beginning, like the thought of his kingship, could have been only a weak presentiment of what was to come.

Beyond his poor prayers, we said, there was, at first, but little in his manner or speech to arouse the suspicion of his soundness. But, in the course of time, the authorities had more certain grounds for alarm. Drs. Benjamin Tightcreed and Oratone Buzz having heard from the lips of one Singleface, an officious student, that Malcolm was a heretic of the deepest dye, summoned him to answer the charge. The culprit was straightway ushered into the mystic presence of these dread inquisitors, and questioned as to his precise views on the vicarious atonement, about which he had spoken, they affirmed, in irreverent terms. However, he had the presence of mind to say that he was as yet somewhat uncertain about his theological position, but hoped erelong to give them an exact statement of his views. Upon this he was informed by the speaker that, while they had the warmest appreciation of free thought, they felt it their duty to cry halt when and wherever the efficacy of Jesus' atoning sacrifice was concerned. For, as Dr. Tightcreed forcibly stated, " nothing is more dangerous in this age of rash statement and unsettled conviction than the smallest aspersion on that infallible means of redemption."

The culprit replied : " I glory in the essential truth of religion, as visible in the lives of all good and great men, and do not see why you should insist so strenuously on a mere dogma which, however essential to ignorant minds, is not required for one who can be trusted to think freely."

Upon this the solemn conclave exchanged looks of pain and alarm, and Oratone Buzz informed him that he was on the road to destruction, and that unless he took the advice of the Evangelist he would rue the day. He attempted to reply, but his voice was drowned by Dr. Buzz, who arose in the heat of his zeal, and spake as follows : " To your knees, audacious boy ! not three months in the college, yet you dare to dispute the Word of God, as given you by the lawful guardians of the Faith ! "

" I have as good a right as either Calvin or Luther, Butler or Beecher, to say what I think, seeing that I do so honestly. This is a question with which neither time nor place has anything to do."

"And do you," continued Buzz, "do you, a mere boy, as yet unfamiliar with the doctrines of the Church and the research of professors, presume to know better than we?"

"I do not pretend," replied Malcolm, "to know anything at all, but speak as freely as I think; and, far from contradicting you, I only express my mind as affected by the substance of your doctrine."

Progressive Bungle, D.D., a large, blue-eyed, good-humored gentleman, now spoke for the first time, saying that he, for his part, did not see any harm in the youth, since his idea of free thought did not preclude fellowship with any earnest seeker of the truth. "But, brethren," he added, "do as ye please with him, — as ye think best for the Lord's cause." Here Dr. Benjamin Tightcreed, a stout old gentleman with a red nose, in an advanced stage of spiritual experience, attired in the most rigid black, declared: "Gentlemen, it is needless to discuss the matter with this headstrong youth. Let him suffer the consequences of his petulance. The question of his position, as appears to me, is very simple. Does he, or does he not, accept salvation through the merits of Christ as the Redeemer and the Judge of the world? If he does, well and good; he may stay and receive the benefits of our institution and societies. But if, on the other hand, he does not, let him be driven from the place, lest he scatter the seeds of infidelity among his companions."

At this moment Dr. Lullaby, the vice-president of the college, a mild, soft-featured man with a perpetual smile, intervened to this effect: "It is not, good brethren, worth our while to concern ourselves about the extravagances of this young man, since they are only the gleams peculiar to visionary youth. And let us remember, all things considered, that he is not alone in the frail boat of heresy. Nor is he at all likely not to outgrow his doubts, considering the utter foolishness of differing from the standard authorities. Just observe," and the Rev. gentleman waxed eloquent, "how unprofitable heresy is! how infinitesimally little a person can gain by adopting the self-sufficient notions and the pretentious infidelity of the period! So, friends, let us be patient and sympathizing to the extent of our ability with those unfortunates who, unable to appreciate the blessings of Christianity, reject them for self-indulgence in a dismal intuitionalism and opaque transcendentalism. Such Utopianism may serve to amuse the unoccupied minds of tailors and in-door workers; but those who subject themselves to the tear and wear of the world require something more palpable."

This remark was as oil to the troubled waters. Tightcreed was pacified, Bungle gratified; and Oratone Buzz smiled as he rose, and said, " Retire, my dear boy, to the silence of the closet, and pray for the help which you so sorely need; and, when you resume your studies, avoid, as you would the wrath to come, the perils of German philosophy, the heathenism of Gœthe, and the paganism of Carlyle. Consider how eminently calculated the genius of Brother Lullaby to improve your prospects of being a successful minister and a worthy son-in-law of my friend Crisp."

Malcolm bowed himself out, deeply impressed by the last words of Dr. Buzz, and for the first time he began to enjoy himself as a respectable member of society, with somewhat less regard, however, for the great men he had worshiped in the silence of the closet. But not till the great theatres of Huberton were opened for the revival of the religion of the country did he discover whether he or the whole Christian world were the bigger fool. The neglect of his studies, however, was in part occasioned by the arrival of Mr. Crisp and his daughter, who came to pass a few weeks in Huberton. They introduced him to many nice people, and in the gayety of the moment he ceased to think about himself. Not till Miss Crisp left for home did he have a minute's serious talk with her. It was to this effect : —

"Now, Malcolm," said that young lady, with an unusually solemn air, rather foreign to her character, "I want you to be as good and religious as you possibly can ; for papa has been hearing strange things of you. You know he cannot bear those dreadful free-thinkers. Before he left home he turned off Mr. Snoozletalk for leaving the Orthodox Church, and joining the Free Religious Society of Bragville. Of course, you know his little peculiarity in this respect. Now, while I would not have you — no, not for the world — fail to tell the truth, don't, as you love me, say anything out of the way."

"What way?" asked Malcolm, archly.

"You know right well what I mean," said the ingenuous maiden.

"Out of the old-fashioned way, you mean, don't you?"

"Well, what if I do?" said the young lady, defiantly. "Is it not the best way there is?"

"I do not say that it is not; but you will at least grant that, judging from the catechism, it is rather a questionable way."

"Yet, for all that, it may be better than a great many others. Do you believe in planchette and the psychometer? Miss Flippert, who took the first prize in algebra, consults the one, and says she sees her future husband through the other. Now, if Julia was a Christian, she would not do such things. People who do not believe in God have great faith in ghosts, it would appear."

"But, Jennie, you do worse things than that. You look at your future life through the death and resurrection of some*body* who lived near two thousand years ago. There's a psychometer for you."

"Oh, you impious fellow, papa would be very angry if he heard you talk so! What do you mean?"

"I only want you to look at the future life through the psychometer of your own thought."

"So I do; but the thought of Christ is great, and I would require a magnifying glass to see it through mine. But, Malcolm, I will trust you; be careful and good." And they parted for the present.

## XIV.

### THE SPECTRE PARTY.

"THE soul is immortal," says the reader. "And so say I," echoes Inverse Vision, a poor radical fowl predestined, perhaps, to make a dinner for some fox of a critic; "for, enthroned as I am in the Hub of the Universe, where comets and stars of all imaginable magnificence spin around me in endless succcession, how can I shut my eyes to the eternity that is revealed in each? Here I sit in just sufficient shade to see those fire-works of God shoot forth in all their native splendor, and splinter, at last, as they culminate, into rainbow rings of glory before they expire on the pale breast of the morning. Tarry with me, O my brother, for one short moment, for I would fain refresh thy sight with the pageantry of the Spirit. But what awful change is this? Thick clouds have gathered, and it were well to take refuge in yonder ruin. What a weird old house is this, with its broken pillars and dilapidated arches! Yet how young it seems when I recall the tides of generations which ebbed and flowed before it was left like a pebble on the beach! And so I dream the past, and see the present; and meanwhile the dream blends with the vision to the transfiguration of all things. The ruin dissolves; and behold, in its place, the wide perspective of an illuminated hall. Yet even here a motley throng of phantoms evolve themselves, and glide gaily or wag adroitly across the polished floors. It is not a dim, sepulchral light that envelops me now ; nor do shrouds shield the bones of the spectres from my gaze. The moonlight yields to the gas-glare of the Christian sociable, and the bones gleam in the gorgeous apparel of the ball ; for Dr. Lullaby is the ghostly pastor of the ghosts. Hark ! the necropolitan festivity begins with a prayer, and a thousand spectral fans pat responsive to its exquisite rhythm. 'All flesh is grass,' I hear the spectre pastor cry ; and after that the words, ' Let the dead bury their dead,' roll rumbling on the floor, and reverberate grimly in his hollow wicker-work of bone. I now recall the real artillery of God, and marvel much at the exceeding great ghostliness of the speech. Yet I marvel still more as the votaries of Fashion interblend, and lose each his personality in confused circles of satin and silk, of velvet and coral, of diamond and flounce, the green interblending with the gold, the drab with the purple, and the pink with the pale, — a perfect chaos of broken rainbows in softest collision : children of Death playing with peacocks' feathers on their father's hell-lit tombs ; a Catherine-wheel revolving furiously on the cross of Christ or on the edge of the gallows. But is there no sign of reality here ? None ; for even Malcolm, at this time, is among the dead. He looks, like the rest, with admiration on that great progressive, Dr. Lullaby, the pivot of this whirling beauty, — the father, son, and particularly the ghost of the rainbow all in one, — and wishes, in his ghostliness, to give up all, and follow him. 'Bestow upon us, O Sun of Righteousness,' he hears him pray, 'the rays of thy wisdom and love; for, poor worms that we are, we long to be warmed into new Life in thee.'

"O poor ghosts, what horrible sins have caused you to so haunt the Church of Fashion, and intrude thus your dismal faces in the vision of living men?" And the Rev. Mr. Treacherous Chin, an old ghost in the stiffest of collars, replies, Because I prefer the 'primrose path' of expedient sin, while my brother there, Mr. Sanctimonious Lip in his new carryall, chooses the 'steep and thorny road that leads to Heaven.'

"O ye seas, that catch to your hearts whole herds of bedeviled swine, look well to your sky-reflecting faces, for horrible things come to the surface after a while! And O ye plains, which reproduce the eternal stars in your flowerets, look well to your soil, for many a bitter seed is sown with the sweet! Avaunt, ye grisly phantoms of the day! yet yield, ere ye go, your spirit-photographs to your friends in the flesh. Mr. Common Vision will now relieve us by finishing."

Dr. Lullaby greets his friends as they come, taking care not to repel those whose conscious looks betray them not to be quite *bon ton*, yet to treat the influentials with adequate respect. He smiles a most captivating smile: "Good evening, Mrs. Furblow. Good evening, Miss Furblow and Miss Fanny. Dear me! this is a surprise. I thought you were still in Europe, Mrs. Furblow, with Mr. —"

"Oh!" replied that lady, "we returned a few days ago. We really had to come and attend to our girls here: they do so need a mother's care. For their sake we had to give up the Pope, Florence, and Naples, and much else."

"But you can return soon," said the doctor, sympathetically, "with your fair blossoms here,"— his eye falling admiringly upon the fresh, violet-eyed faces of the dear girls, who were gaily decked out in blue silk and Valenciennes.

"Oh, yes, Dr. Lullaby," chimed in Miss Fannie, who was sixteen and very enthusiastic. "We should admire to go. I wish ma would take us right away. But there!" (assuming a serious tone) "we would have to give up your nice sermons. They have done us a great deal of good."

"I am rejoiced to hear it," said his puissance affectionately, only a slight shade of unction discernible in his tone, and was going to add something about being a humble instrument, &c., in the hands of the Lord, when Miss Furblow told him that that book, "Christ in the Soul," he had lent her was a treasure, and that she had cried over it, but still there were one or two things which she did not quite understand.

Upon this his puissance said to her, as one having authority, "Knock, and it shall be opened unto you. Any thing that I can do to help you will be most cheerfully done. I am always at home to the anxious inquirer. I shall expect to see you soon." Then, turning to the mother, he added, "Verily the soil should be often stirred round young plants in the Lord."

A young gentleman by the name of Fitzsnibbert,

who had been twirling his moustache behind an adjoining pillar, hearing this dialogue, pulled in a long breath, and muttered, as he discharged it, "What would I not give for the Jovinian delight of converting those belles? I must think seriously of entering the ministry." Malcolm, who was also in the vicinage, thought this valiant knight could find, if he tried, a more worthy occupation for his arms.

Mrs. Furblow was charmed by the tender interest the eminent clergyman took in her "dears," and, becoming confidential, entertained him with an account of her symptoms; for her ladyship suffered much from that polite demon called Dyspepsia, — while the young ladies looked about, either ruminating on the state of their souls, or, what is more likely, upon the selection of their periodical silk, which was suggested by the aspect of the millinery of the other "divinities" around them.

Then the musical entertainment commenced, and, notwithstanding the excellence thereof, for it was the best the city could afford, many who had not even opened their lips before took this opportunity to evince a remarkable loquacity. Mrs. Furblow withdrawn, his puissance, unconsciously adapting himself to the next on hand, a big, burly individual with a tomahawk nose and a face to match, cried, "How goes it, Bottleton? This chilly spell is good for your business."

"Sure enough, Lullaby! fourteen thousand, eight hundred and eighty-eight gallons a day of the pure and unadulterated. There is something for Gough to handle."

"Ah, I am ashamed of you, Brother Bottleton; all that I can say or do, you won't give up that distillery and go in for the Lord. Come, now, be good. You know it is far beneath you," he said in persuasive tones, smiling the while. He rarely spoke so authoritatively on morality as applicable to certain individuals as on the tenderness of the Deity; and he thought the Divine Love, as manifest in fond personal sympathy and communion with others, should be indulged in at all hazards, even if some of the stricter sentiments of the Sermon on the Mount occasionally suffered during the acts of indulgence. What was the Messiah for, if not to soften the rigor of the Ten Commandments with the leniency peculiar to him in his mediatorial capacity between God and such sinners as Lullaby and his constituents?

"I don't know anything of the kind, Lullaby," cried Bottleton with the grimmest of smiles. "My spirit is just like the Unitarian God, perfectly good to the temperate, but the Devil himself to the intemperate. No, no, friend, you can't catch me there. Good spirits are not to be sneered at. By the way, you like that Burgundy of mine. Come sup with me to-morrow. Bungle will be there; and Buzz wants to taste my Providence." (Oysters, it is to be hoped).

"Thanks, thanks, my friend; but ah, so busy, you see, — so busy. Let you know to-morrow."

Malcolm, meanwhile, was busy wondering what Nebuchadnezzar would have done had the three Jews said, "Now, Nebuchadnezzar, we are inclined to believe that this new golden god of yours is not such a good thing after all. Come, now, be decent, and order it to be taken away. We will give you a much better one in its place." Nebuchadnezzar was not so much to blame; he believed in his accustomed god until the existence of a better was practically demonstrated to him. Bottleton actually felt that his spirits were as productive of good as the one whose operation he saw around him, and he spoke from his heart. The soil does not require to be stirred round those old plants in the Lord, — oh, no!

"How are you, Brother Stoppleton?" asked his puissance, turning to a meek-faced little man who looked as if he rued the cost of his religion more than his want of it (he had just been complaining to a friend that it cost him a thousand a year, and that, had it not been for the wife, he would have given it up long ago). After Stoppleton had informed him that he was pretty well, Dr. Lullaby then asked how that little fellow of his was who had been sick of the measles, and conversed sympathetically with him.

Dr. Lullaby next caught the eye of a handsome, elegantly dressed, middle-aged man, with long side whiskers, and an air which indicated refinement, yet of a sort rarely seen outside of certain galaxies of fashion. This person accosted his minister in low, melodious tones, — indeed, in tones so melodious that even Dr. Lullaby's seemed momentarily surpassed. "Aw, my dear Lullaby," he began, affectionately stroking his pet whisker, "you look jaded, — the fault, possibly, of your lecture yester eve."

"Do I, Mr. Tulip? But speaking rarely fatigues me."

"How fortunate you are!" exclaimed Mr. Tulip, with a look of admiration. "You must have an enviable system. Indeed, your quiet candor, interwoven as it ever is with extreme geniality of sentiment, can only come from a sound constitution, pervaded by a Christian spirit. And your success as a thinker, also, considering the demands of society on your time, and your unflagging attention to the afflicted, has far exceeded the hopes of your flock."

"Do not, I beg of you, exaggerate my small ability: I have but poorly done the little task appointed me, although, to be sure, the vast spread of infidelity which attended the preaching of Theodore Parker has taxed my energies to the utmost. Before him, hardly any one dared to doubt the letter of Revelation. But now, alas! not a day passes without an alarm peal from the Church tower, calling us to arms. And so wily and daring — so very wily and daring — is the foe, that we experience some difficulty in locating and keeping a fixed line of defense. The radicalism of the day, not content with cannonading the Church, actually threatens to abolish the State, — yes, Mr. Tulip, to abolish the State, and give us up to the unbridled license of the vulgar."

"Frightful, frightful!" exclaimed Mr. Tulip, turning pale, and nervously catching the end of a whisker reaching to his vest pocket. "But you may exaggerate the evil, Dr. Lullaby. I take comfort in the thought that even among the radicals there are a few tender and beautiful spirits which must, in a large degree, atone for the unfeeling and flippant character of many. To satisfy a pardonable curiosity, I went to one of their gatherings, — the most select, you know, — and was surprised at the pious tone of the discussion. Although nominally anti-Christian, much of the conversation was essentially correct, and I was greatly pleased with it. Now, if such a truly spiritual reaction as this, Dr. Lullaby, is going to succeed the bitter infidelity of Theodore Parker, and counteract the demoniac wit of John Know, the Church has little to fear from radicals."

"I agree with you quite. I admire piety even in a radical, and deem it good for our cause that such characters as you first mentioned should rise to leaven the coarse matter of infidelity. It will greatly facilitate our victory. But beware, Mr. Tulip, beware of giving your confidence too rashly, of opening your heart too freely, to any of those who bear a name so suggestive of unfaithfulness to the Lamb, so repugnant to him who has suffered for his ungrateful children. Christianity, in this hour of peril, expects every man to do his duty."

"Yes, Doctor," replied Mr. Tulip, with a sigh, relinquishing the whisker. "It is well to avoid even the appearance of sin."

On this they both sauntered in to supper.

What a magnificent table lay spread before the hungry throng, or the throng that was supposed to be hungry! Decalcomino had done his utmost for the faithful few. What a brilliant array of variegated ice-creams! what a phalanx of oysters, scalloped, fried, and broiled, entrenched by lofty tureens of chicken salad, and commanded by pyramids of the most inviting cake! "Oh, my!" as a young school-marm, who had come to the feast as the guest of a rich friend, exclaimed to her frosty-nosed little brethren at home, "it was perfectly splendid! It gives me a sick-headache to think of it." What a clatter of knives, forks, spoons, and plates, and what a spreading of napkins! what a display of devoted attention on the part of the males! and what sweet nonchalance visible on the faces of the females!

"This is far beyond Knox's Presbyterianism!" exclaimed Malcolm, bringing to mind the frigid tea and coarse oat-cake he had enjoyed at the *soirées* of his former kirk. "But somehow," he mused, "the Hubertonians do not seem a great deal better for the greater prodigality of Providence with the aid of Decalcomino in their behalf. These young ladies are not so stout and healthy as my old friends on the other side. Those hot furnaces, those horse-cars and carriages, are not conducive to strength of limb, and this luxurious fare to strength of digestion. Yet, upon the whole, I like the heads and faces of these girls better than those of the Darklyn; and how much better their manners are! Still there is a lack of vitality about them that I do not understand: they do not enjoy life so much as they might be made to. I wish folk were more faithful to the Hebrew religion, and paid attention to that of the Greeks. How much better balanced the culture of the latter! They gave as much attention to the body as they did to the mind. Hence the wonderful harmony visible in all their productions. Christianity has been comparatively one-sided. It has made the flesh the home of the Devil and his angels, and treated it as such even unto this evening," — and he looked upon the pious throng as it precipitated itself upon the indigestible, and in surfeiting itself therewith, sowed the seeds of future distress.

Even Mrs. Furblow forgot her symptoms, and her dear girls the amount of Christ they had in their souls, and joined in the attack on the viands. But what does it matter about a nightmare or two or about a slight inactivity of the liver, as long as one is possessed of the sweet consciousness of being on the road to salvation? We would like a sermon for a change on the text that the kingdom of Hell is a mustard-seed as well as that of Heaven. Our experience teaches us that both have their root in the same being, and are equally susceptible of cultivation, the one of becoming the tree of Life, and the other the tree of Death. There is some truth in what Pluffle said, after all, "A serious hour in the midst of gaiety does not always come amiss."

Good night.

# BOOK II.

RAINBOW AND REALITY.

# I.

## DEACON CRISP AND HIS DEVIL.

"I AM glad to say, Brother Pluffle," said Mr. Crisp, on his return home from Huberton, "that Lawson begins to grow decidedly Christian."

"Well, Deacon Crisp, perhaps you were right about him, after all. But, if I may speak my mind, I must repeat that there is a nameless something in him that grates a little on my nerves. It is not irreverence, nor is it downright impiety, but evidently a positive want, or, at all events, something quite out of the way. You said, if I remember aright, that his prayers were poor."

"Oh, you are too hard to please, Pluffle. Young men will be young men, and Malcolm is wonderful, considering that he is entirely self-taught. You cannot expect him to acquire at once that Christian sweetness and serene dignity which even the best of us sometimes lack. 'Tis true, I was extremely sorry that he did not incline to prayer; but that note of Lullaby's reassures me, and I do most sincerely hope he will give us no more trouble on that score."

"Yes, brother, it behooveth us to have faith. But for my part"—

"Is there no end to these 'buts' of yours, Pluffle?"

"Excuse me, sir: I was about to say, that, since

my interests are yours, I would feel more at ease in regard to Mr. Lawson if Tightcreed and Graves were as favorable to him as Lullaby, who, I grieve to observe, displays a marked regard for Universalism, manifesting itself in a shocking leniency to Radicalism, that insidious Infidelity already become so fashionable in Upper Peanut and Special Culture Streets."

"You astonish me: I thought Lullaby was quite sound."

"Well, so do many." Here Pluffle looked very mysterious. "But faithful adherence to the Word often compels us to differ from the crowd. However, I only give you my opinion of the man, and let it go at that. Doctors will differ, you know, and the best of us are liable to misapprehension. Rest assured, if I did not esteem it a pastoral duty to have an eye on the possible foes of our own household, I would not bring so influential a personage into question."

"Your eye is very sharp," said Crisp.

"Far be it from me to say aught against Dr. Lullaby as a well-meaning gentleman; but, alas! Infidelity nowadays is so insidious in its attacks on the heart that I am constantly dreading a surprise,— yes, Brother Crisp, a surprise. We may consider ourselves in a state of siege, and Dr. Lullaby, you know, has but recently entered the walls of our denomination, whereas Graves and Tightcreed are old and tried friends, who bid fair to control the destinies of the country."

"There may be some sense in that, Pluffle. But

how is it that you, who are so sound yourself, should prefer those men to Lullaby? He is quite equal to them. I have always thought myself a pretty good judge, and my experience is that ministers are not unlike horses: I have yet to find one that is perfectly kind and sound." And the deacon chuckled over his own wit.

"Well, I suppose," said Pluffle, smiling grimly, "that your judgment is fully equal to mine. But"—

"Oh, those 'buts,' Pluffle."

"Deacon Crisp, if you intend to insult me, you certainly succeed."

"Pardon me, brother: I will be more careful."

"This treatment is altogether unexpected from you, sir. A trusted pastor who opens his heart to one of his flock ought not to be sneered at in this way."

"Perhaps I'm wrong, Pluffle: but, believe me, the possible treachery of a Lullaby is nothing at all beside the wanton Infidelity of the masses and the shameless wickedness of the country. That is what appalls me; and how to put a stop to it exercises me night and day. Now, if you can help me there, I will be much obliged."

"That is just what exercises me, also," cried Pluffle enthusiastically. "It has cost me endless prayer and many a sleepless night. Let us prepare for immediate descent on the Enemy. He occupies the theatres, and there is where the decisive battle for Christ must be fought. Once possessed of that stronghold of Satan, we will turn the fire of his great guns against himself, and he shall yield to the lightnings of the Lord. 'Gospel for the poor! Gospel for the masses!' Let that be our watchword and battle-cry."

This speech went to the deacon's heart, and he shook Pluffle's hand, asking pardon for his momentary aberration.

Next Sunday Malcolm went to the Huberton Theatre, and found it occupied by the advanced guard of Christianity. But there was no enemy to meet it, for the rich admirers of the knights, who fought the devils underneath, obtained the best seats, so that the "poor" had to go off and break the Sabbath elsewhere, or sit as near "the gods" as possible, — namely, within an inch of the roof.

## II.

### THE NOISELESS STRUGGLE.

WHO are the genuine fighters of the Fiend? Numerous ghosts fill the room in reply, and we cannot away from the piteous spectacle. "O mother, with the sunken eyes and the dark rims round them, thrice waked out of thy deep sleep to tend the suffering babe that vice or other incapacity has foisted upon thee! O toiler of the deep, who hast just left the skin of thy horny palm on the frozen rigging aloft, and now gropest thy way to thy dark and noisome recess below! O thief of the night, and even thou, O woman of the town, who this moment takest thy doleful walk in the drizzling rain! and all ye who seek, and perhaps vainly, to burrow your way out of the Bastiles wherein your own follies, or those of society have pent you up! it is you that fight with the Fiend. But who is there to sing your victories, and encourage you to persevere? What is called your filth is often your sweetness, and ye perish in it for the luxury of others, like bees, or like the young trees that, being overshadowed by a more vigorous growth, wither and rot that the latter may live the better. To you we owe, for aught we know, as deep a debt of gratitude as we do to our prophets and bards; and shall we content ourselves with beating the air for other's amusement, or wasting the paper on which we write?

Gospel for the poor! Mrs. Winslow's Soothing Syrup for the poor, or some such ready-made convenient decoction, instead of our lives, instead of hard, genuine work in their behalf, in short, tall talk about Christ, instead of being Christs ourselves. Be little Christs, exhorts a great preacher.* No: be great ones, is the constant cry of the soul, as it bids us see the possibility of that being in the history of our kind, or bids the trees of the forest teach it to us; for the perennial fall of their fruits and of their leaves, and lastly themselves, go to enrich the soil that is the commonwealth of their kind. To-morrow we may die, and leave our little ones to the world and its mercies; the better we have treated it, the better able it to take care of them. Let this thought, if so be that we love not the Truth for the sake of itself, move us to be up and doing,—doing while it is yet day; "for the night cometh when no man can work."

\* "*Be little Christs, if I may say so,*" was the cautious advice of a distinguished lecturer on preaching to the students at Yale. (Yale Lecturing on Preaching, by Beecher, p. 66.)

## III.

### HIS FRIEND SHAFT.

MALCOLM saw at a glance that every person must answer for himself the great questions of Science and Religion. "For my part," he said, "I see nothing but mystery and mystery in this world, and do what I will, I cannot escape the conviction that I am immortal. It is true that I am wretchedly ignorant, but, strange to say, nobody tells me anything that I do not know already, except facts of observation and experience, about which it is not worth while to dispute. But in regard to gods we have nothing but myth and tradition, and, to be frank, I think, if I put my mind to it, I could tell some pretty big stories myself. Still, there are quite enough of them already, and no doubt in the hands of the Truthful they will make the best illustrations of Eternal Wisdom."

But what was Brother Crisp to say to this radical effusion? Malcolm did not realize his circumstances till the theatre preaching took place, and then the struggle between his conscience or reason and his desire for immediate individual gratification commenced. But he still remained the docile pupil, seizing with avidity, and arranging intuitively, the facts that came to hand. It was hard, indeed, for him, as will be seen hereafter, to overlook the brilliant prospects Mr. Crisp had painted for him. But Truth was on his side, although we are sorry to say it did not prevail so much at first. Had he been pleased to subordinate it, he might have become a member of the circus company aforesaid, and thus made himself most acceptable to his patron. For the moment he was only astonished at the above phenomenon.

About this time he was introduced to a person by the name of Shaft. This was a man about forty years old, who was noted for his somewhat eccentric yet very radical views. Amused by the character of Malcolm's humor, which had a certain resemblance to his own, he deigned to make his acquaintance.

Peter Shaft lived alone in the topmost story of a lofty house, in unpleasant proximity to a tarred roof and sundry organ grinders whose serenades he loved to interrupt. Nobody knew whether he were rich or poor, or how he contrived to exist. He was supposed, however, to be "pretty well off," as he evidently had enough to live without working for the sake of money,—and a little to give away.

Although he possessed the reputation of great literary talent, and, on account of his critical acumen, was often consulted by young authors, nobody had seen any of his writings,—that is, if he had ever been weak enough to indulge in the luxury of expressing himself on paper. For it really is a luxury to write, as soon as the habit is formed; and few can afford it. It is almost as pleasant as preaching, however good the voice of the aspiring evangelist,— but nothing like as pleasant as praying. "For," as a friend of ours lately told us, "far from having any difficulty in praying, it is the hardest thing in the world for me to stop after I have once fairly begun." Now as we can on a pinch lay aside the pen, we must grant that praying is the pleasanter occupation of the two. The habit of writing is apt to grow upon one like tobacco smoking, and ought to be kept in check. We certainly know such to be the case with talking, whether within or without the doors of the Church. "Did you ever hear me preach?" asked Coleridge of Lamb. "I never heard you do anything else," was the immediate response. Joking aside, how happy those must be who get thousands and thousands per annum for indulging in their favorite propensities! Says Patrick, "It beats Banagher, and Banagher beats the Divil."

Mr. Shaft knew his weakness, and stood as clear of the pen, as regard for his uncommon philosophical idea would permit him. Therefore his genius, if he had such a troublesome thing, had to content itself with speech when he happened, which was not often, to find a suitable victim. Then it would be poured forth with so much vehemence and power that the astonished individual that had invoked it would feel like the grocery clerk, who, having given a strong twitch to the string in the tin bottle on the counter, pulls out yards more than he can use.

He was a tall, meagre individual, with a slight cast in his deep hazel eyes. For the rest, he did not differ much in appearance from the rest of his kind, save in having on each side of his somewhat wide mouth a singular network of dimples, which was evidently the result of indulgence in hearty laughter. Yes, notwithstanding his absorbing appreciation of the sublime, Mr. Shaft was remarkably fond of good jokes, and was not above the invention of the same. Nor did he, in the absence of sympathizing friends, fail to laugh at them himself, especially when entirely alone. So radically eccentric was he in this, that his neighbors entertained serious doubts concerning his perfect sanity. In the middle of the night they were often startled by the singular sounds emanating from his solitary apartment.

Strange to say, in view of the above, Mr. Shaft had been very unfortunate. He lost his wife and two beautiful children by railway accident some years before this time. People wondered at the stoicism he evinced under this affliction, and some gave him the credit of being hard-hearted. But we knew better. He loved Eternal Truth, and subordinated all other loves to the love of it. Hence he was always cheerful. Speaking of his bereavement, he said, "I can realize how Jesus felt when he said, 'Who is my mother, and who are my brethren?' I seek to be worthy of a similar family, — namely, that of the obedient to the laws of nature or of God. I do not care which of the two words you use."

"Why," said we, "that's Pantheism!"

"Call it anything you like," he replied. "To me it is a positive increase of Life."

Therefore Mr. Shaft was a happy man, and lived

on, doing his best for himself and others. Malcolm entered his room one day, and informed him that he could not accept the doctrine of Vicarious Atonement, as given him by his teachers.

"That is unfortunate," rejoined Shaft, smiling. "What is the difficulty?"

"I cannot reconcile it with Nature's method of compensation, according to which every sin involves certain punishment, and every act of virtue sufficient reward. Sin is a fire, and there is no salvation for the burned, however great the past effort of God to save us, unless it be in such realization of the badness of sin that we fly from it in horror."

"True, in the main," said Mr. Shaft. "But before we venture to discuss this formidable doctrine of yours, let us come to some understanding in regard to our relative positions, in order that we may avoid unprofitable antagonism. You, as an orthodox student, conceive Christ to be God, either in deference to the dictates of your own Reason, or to those of the spirit of Authority and Tradition. Yet, be this as it may, you will be content, for the time being at least, to turn away from the latter that you may better hearken to the former."

"I have no difficulty in so doing," said the youth.

"So much the better," said Mr. Shaft, with increased stateliness of tone. "Now, then, the foundation of a profitable conversation being laid, it is well to remember that, inasmuch as you and I have had different experiences of life, we must of necessity see things from different stand-points. If, for instance, you stood upon a pinnacle of the Temple of Knowledge, you would see immeasurably more than if you stood only at the porch. Suppose, now, a person who had led a pure and holy life in a world much superior to this, in point of moral culture, chanced to light on the earth, would he not — so great were the contrast between the two spheres — think himself in Hell?"

"Yes, if he were not too much of an optimist. But to be quite frank, Mr. Shaft, I am not in a decided state about anything. My imagination gives me no peace, and, flying over all creation with me, seems bent on dashing out my brains against the moons of Metaphysics. Your composure, however, gives me a moment of rest, and I am glad to listen."

"Well, in regard to vicarious sacrifice, let us look as deeply as we can into that most suggestive idea. You alluded, in the first place, to the past effort of God to save us. Now that is partial. The effort of God always is, and it consists, we may say, in his enabling us to make the realization you specified. Most people dwell wholly in the dark, and only occasionally catch a glimpse of the Kingdom of Light. And the Son of Man, who appears like a flash of lightning, illuminating the world from one end to the other, is a ray from that Kingdom. In contemplating the character of that ray, and in looking at my world in the light afforded by it, I see that God appears to suffer for the wicked."

"Appears to suffer, you say. How can you, a radical, connect the thought of suffering with the Divine Person?"

"Have patience. I am more orthodox than you, although I am not the hired advocate of a sect. See here: if there are Infinite Holiness and Health in the universe, do these not seem to be accompanied by Infinite Sickness and Distress?"

"Yes."

"Well, shall not the Divine Person be the Lord and Master over the Kingdom of Hell as well as over that of Heaven?"

"Certainly."

"To this end, then, he specially manifests himself in the person of Jesus of Nazareth, in order to establish his government of Love over the still wild country of Sin and Death."

"And not over the Strength and Beauty of the universe?"

"No: for his beneficial rule has been already acknowledged by the true genius of all past time in philosophy and in art, in agriculture and in mechanics, in the freedom of our Scandinavian ancestors, and in the reverent worship of the Hebrews. In short, Jesus comes to call sinners, not the righteous, to repentance."

"Positively, you are more orthodox than Dr. Buzz himself. But why should the manifestation of God be special in the case of Jesus, and not so in mine?"

"I do not say that it is not special in yours. If, according to Calvin, there is no good in us save what we receive by the grace of God, I should certainly say that goodness in you is the same as it is in Jesus. But I am more orthodox than Calvin. God suffers for the sins of the world in so far as he, being Infinite Love, sympathizes with all persons and things in their efforts to improve themselves and others. 'I and my Father are one,' are the grandest words ever uttered by him. Many people receive the impression that Jesus was a very unhappy person. But, far from thinking that, he himself exclaims on his way to Calvary, 'Weep not for me, daughters of Jerusalem, but for yourselves and your children. For if they do these things unto a green tree, what shall be done to a dry?' Now while I grant, with Novalis, that there is Infinite Melancholy in religion, I know that it contains Infinite Joy. How can the enthusiastic worship of Truth be other than the most blessed thing conceivable? Therefore, in the better sense of the word Self, Jesus was anything but a self-sacrificing man. Who would not gladly give the shadow for the reality, the inferior for the superior? or who would not perish like a dry acorn for the sake of becoming a green oak? or, as illustrated, also, in the parable of the talents, who would not use his money for the sake of increase? Thus Jesus, it is plain, lost his life to save it, even in this world; for what are Time and Space to the Divine Person?"

Malcolm hoped that they were not quite useless. And Mr. Shaft continued, in still statelier tones: "Now if Jesus, while on earth, remained perfectly true to himself, — so true, indeed, that he did not require, as did the prodigal son, to come to himself before he could return to his Father, — his crucifixion — had it not been for the ghastly spectacle which made him cry out, 'Father, forgive them, they know not what they do!'—must have been the crowning joy of his life, the consummation of his heavenly task, although, in reality, it may only have been the burning of the ship which brought him to another world infinitely more worth conquering than this."

"According to you, then, it is impossible for one to die for the world's good."

"Quite, unless he is a rascal, a mere body, so given to the love of pleasure that he will not strive for anything higher. For God, as manifest in any person, is there for the sole purpose of conquering Sin and Death for his own *Re-creation*, the renewing or regeneration of those individuals who love and suffer with him for the good of others; and in so far as those individuals succeed in helping others, the world through them becomes more satisfactory to God. Such, then, is the Atonement, as seen in the light of Jesus' life. Death, says Fichte, is nothing, existing only in the dead gaze of the dead beholder. And the suffering of the Divine Person is chiefly the infinite compassion inspired by the disorder and distress which he, as represented not only by the wonderful Nazarene, but by every other honest person, comes to lessen and alleviate; and so infinite is this sympathy, that it reaches even the worst denizens of Hell."

"Hell!"

"Yes: because all below Divinity is Hell, and the loving kindness of God is infinite. Nor sparrow nor hawk falleth to the ground without his sanction. Satan himself is only a fallen angel; and what, pray, are you and I? Have we not fallen?"

So weird was the expression of his friend's eye, that Malcolm shrank from the question, and replied with another: "But how do you reconcile God's love for Devils with Jesus' hatred for Pharisees?"

"He regarded them as quite dead, — so dead that he only introduced them into his pictures of life as so much black paint, on the principle that stars shine only in the dark. And so intense was his realization of their utter nothingness, that he called them graves, over which one walked without even knowing that they were there."

"But this is a roundabout way of getting at the truth of dead doctrines."

".True. But if those effete doctrines were once alive with truth, their souls live forever."

"Yet the fault I find with your views is that they take away from the reality of wretchedness and sin, since they imply that these have only a phenomenal existence. For my part, I agree with the Hebrew prophet in thinking it is a fearful thing to be in the hands of the living God."

"If words take me away from reality, they always bring me back. It may, indeed, be a fearful thing for you to be in those hands; but it is far otherwise with me. And as to wretchedness and woe having *only* phenomenal existence, why, even that is too much."

"You bring me beyond my depth. According to you all the false doctrines of the Church may be truths in disguise."

"Yes: therefore, as you value your talents, waste them not in the refutation of theological errors. For these rest, as Goethe says, on the conviction that the false is true. Yet, on the other hand, since it will not do to connive at falsehood, let us state and keep stating what is true for ourselves, and it will be the loving embrace of the morning of knowledge. All errors refute themselves, even while they refute one another. And in this way the truth is gradually evolved, and every sect blends with its neighbor, so that in time reason and harmony take the places of discord and dissension. If names be any criterion, the world is perfect; for the truly orthodox are truly liberal, the truly Catholic truly Protestant, the truly radical truly conservative, the truly Christian truly religious, — I was going to say, truly freely religious; but double-barreled adverbs are dangerous."

"But look at the reality, Mr. Shaft, — my reality."

"I don't wish to see it. However, to oblige you, I will descend to your level, and look from the porch of my church. I am now elbowed by two individuals, the self-styled liberal and the conscious church-member. The latter is a snobbish aristocrat, and the former being an ostentatious parvenu, ill-feeling subsists between them. For my part, rather than stand guard over my privileges with a loaded pistol in my hand, or keep offering them to those who do not wish them, I would throw them out the window. However, I am glad to see that the aristocrat is becoming less exclusive, and that the parvenu, experiencing the folly of extravagance, becomes economical."

"You bring to mind Drs. Buzz and Lullaby, who have just joined the I. S. N. D. The one was a close communionist, and the other a liberal Christian. Extremes meet in a most unaccountable manner in this optimistic age. But, by the way, how do you term your system of philosophy?"

"I haven't any."

"What, then, is your aim, your purpose in Life?"

"Work."

"Nothing more?"

"No: for that is the only Heaven we gain in place of the one which has been lost. There is no rest for the wicked, and the blessed see that idleness is the root of all evil. Are you not happiest while engaged in some congenial pursuit, or wrapped in earnest thought?"

"Certainly. I agree with you there. My mind is like the demon with whom a Scotch wizard made a compact. This demon agreed to do everything for him on the condition that he should be supplied with sufficient work; and if the wizard failed to keep him employed, he was to be torn in pieces by the demon. Absence of the true ideas which compel us to work for the good of ourselves, if not for that of others, is the ruin of the soul, and the symbol of that ruin is deformity. How foolish some of us are! I heard Dr. Buzz say, in the pulpit, that if he thought there were no Heaven after death, he would seek all the pleasures of the world."

"I am glad that he has studied spiritual geography to so much advantage. I rather like him. He is a good laugher. Nor is he a useless member of society. Midas must have his compensations. Moreover, weathercocks are useful, — they are the legitimate consequences of steeples as well as of state-houses." Here something seemed to amuse Mr. Shaft so that he laughed boisterously, and Malcolm joined in with him, although he hardly knew what he was laughing at. When they had exhausted themselves, Malcolm rose to go; but Mr. Shaft would not let him depart without taking with him a little essay that he had just composed on the harbinger of the morn, saying, as he gave it to him, "You remember that when the magician you alluded to as having pledged himself to the Evil One found himself unable to supply him with more profitable work, he luckily thought to ask him to make ropes of sand long enough to reach to the moon. This request baffled the Fiend and saved the warlock further anxiety about his future life. Let us apply this to ourselves. The mind must be occupied, and although our writing and our speech may not amount to more than a rope of sand, the honest employment of its energies to the repression of its ever-surging restlessness — even if we be reduced to checkers, chess, cards, definition-making, or other metaphysical fopperies of the times — is our salvation."

# IV.

## THE EVERLASTING PARADOX.

"I DO not care," says Mr. Sweep, "for an artist who only makes a good stroke once in a while. No person ought to draw unless he can keep making them all the time."

But, alas! Mr. Sweep's ideal is far beyond our reach; so we must content ourselves with the inferior pen which strives to illuminate the night of these pages, in utter ignorance whether its attempts will pass for stars or the most abject candles possible. Yet why should we concern ourselves about this? for having long since passed the bounds óf good sense, according to the standard geography of that region, those devout beings, profanely termed critics, who are so full of appreciation of the new, will be so enraptured with the Romeo of this work, that, even before he dies, they will cut him up into little bits, and make every bit a star, so that people will fall in love with night, and hate the day.

Malcolm was so carried away by the influx of ideas which attended his advent in Huberton that he could no more repress himself than if he had a heart as fiery as that of Mount Vesuvius. Yet so concerned were the guardians of the Faith about his spiritual welfare, that, not yet certain of his good intentions, they labored to ensure his thorough conversion. But as the reader, no doubt, — especially if he is a critic, — has himself experienced the agreeable process of revival, he will not require a demonstration of the influences brought to bear on this young man. Omitting, then, the description of that exciting experience, we shall relate how Malcolm endeavored to reciprocate the concern of his teachers by doing all he could in their behalf.

"I like nothing better," he said, "than a warm expression of sentiment; and, if this is the popular remedy for the soul, why should it not be equally good for the mind? For my part, half dead though I am, I will stir up the fires of my heart, and cut myself a passage through the sea of theological confusion. I will, of course, be on the lookout not to collide with those steamers who rejoice in the name of the Lord; yet I am bound to show them some fun."

Thus Malcolm, though he may not have carried the sails of a full-rigged vessel, had motive power of his own to reach the haven of his hope.

"I say, Arthur," he began one day, as that individual lay becalmed after a toilsome passage of Scripture, under the command of Captain Tightcreed, "did it ever occur to you that theology was a pack of cards?"

"No!" cried the astonished student. "I guess you mean your own theology."

"No; I mean that game which, if well played on the magic table of popular superstition, will make the player's fortune."

"And you should avoid," replied Arthur, "that

game which, if well played on the boards of infidelity and atheism, will cheat people out of all genuine religious feeling."

"Yet, how does it happen, Arthur, that the knights of the black cloth are so much better off than those of the green? The bishops have thousands and thousands per annum, and all the leading ones who turn up the trump heart, our Lord, are remarkably well off. To be sure, the small fry of the ministry do not make a great deal; yet neither do the lower classes of gamblers and fortune tellers. It all depends upon the hand. Dr. Lullaby told me his pen was worth a hundred dollars an hour."

"That is wholly untrue; for the instruction given by such as Lullaby is well worth the money, while the gambler stirs up the evil passions to no purpose.

"I suppose," replied Malcolm, "the Southern clergymen did not stir up the passions of the rebels by quoting Scripture in favor of their peculiar institution. Nor am I quite sure that most of the Northern ones were particularly anxious to tone down the nuisance. But I will grant that, in view of the ignorance and dishonesty that abound, the metaphor of the cards is a little too strong. The plague of superstition is not the worst. Last night I had rather a strange vision. It contained a good deal."

"Let us hear it!" said Arthur, glad of his victory.

"I dreamed I stood inside the gates of Heaven, speaking with an angel who sat in a melancholy mood, jingling a bunch of rusty keys. 'How is it,' asked I, astonished to see the gates wide open, — not even ajar, — 'that you have grown so liberal?

I thought you were very particular in these heretical times. I had no idea that I, who can pray so poorly, was to find myself here.'

"'Oh,' said he, smiling, 'here there is a perpetual reformation to correspond with the one below. Nothing but sheer ignorance presumes that we are in any degree exclusive. The only difficulty is to get people to come this way; for the loudest and most showy object to the open gates, and go off elsewhere, saying, This is no place for the elect. We cannot mix with the masses.'"

"That's rather rough, Malcolm; yet I suppose the Lord cannot dispense with the best souls, even if they are tainted a little by heresy."

"Here," continued the visionary, "the angel appeared quite overcome, and burst into tears, when I beheld the most striking phenomenon conceivable. The air of Heaven became illumed by the softest and most beautiful light I ever saw. Diamond mountains, it is said, dissolve in the air when angels weep."

"Is that all?" asked Arthur.

"No, indeed. When the angel recovered himself, I asked him whether many took advantage of their splendid opportunities. He replied with a look of sorrow which pierced me to the core, and, lifting his hand, he pointed to the plains below. I turned round, and beheld a vast sea of all kinds of people, each carrying the banner of his faith in hand. They appeared to come towards us in successive waves; but, as I looked more attentively, some went back, while others went both backwards and forwards, yet advanced upon the whole. I imagined myself again on the Atlantic; for great black clouds would appear in the east, and, spreading themselves over the face of the sky, would burst with loud thunder, and rain balls of fire on the panic-stricken multitude.

"'Why is this?' I asked.

"'That,' he replied, 'is because they gather together in crowds. The smoother the surface and warmer the air of society, the greater the evaporation of sin. After a while, a cold wind blows from the north,— the wind of insincerity,— and few escape uninjured. This, you see, is a city of innumerable gates; yet, so great is the dislike people have of coming alone, that they crush each other in their attempts to enter through the same gate.'

"'Then,' said I, 'you are something of an individualist. You can't be a Christian angel.'

"'I am a universal one,' he said, stiffly. 'I help every person to realize the blessings of Heaven; but, as long as he does only that which his neighbors do, he is apt to ignore the gates of Eternal Life. See that bishop. He leaves this open door, and, turning himself into a comet, sweeps off with a whole host of well-dressed Christians for a tail.'

"'But,' said I, 'he is a bishop still, more than half extinguished by his mitre. How can you call him a comet?'

"'Wait,' he replied, 'till you grow accustomed to the ether. You will soon see that a burning and a shining light may well be an erring body.'"

"You make me think of Swedenborg," said Arthur. "Bad spirits, on approaching the good, emit an offensive odor which drives them back; but I was not aware the odor of respectability had that effect."

"Phariseeism is the besetting sin of respectability. Carlyle was the first to propose the crusade which ought to take place against it."

"Yet you said the Christians who rejected their advantages were well dressed. Carlyle believed so much in good clothes, that he undertook the office of tailor for himself."

"No wonder; for the words of the prophet are realized: 'They parted my garments amongst them, and on my vesture did they cast lots.' If Christ was God, he was also Eternal Thought; and, since language is the garment of all thought, his words must have been his clothes. Thus it would appear that each of the Christian sects had an appropriate piece of the original texture of the gospel, cut and sewed to fit the configuration of each religious body."

"But the coat, the principal garment of Christ, being without seam, remains whole."

"To be sure. Hence the gambling of the church. Even we must assist in casting lots for it. But here is the sublimest thought of all: a millennium is at stake."

"A millennium!"

"Yes: your millennium and mine; and it all depends upon the clothes we wear: but the mystery of the seamless coat is beyond our reach. It is indeed easy to secure a remnant of gospel truth; but the whole still remains to be appropriated by him who is equal to the task."

"But every theologian is apt to think that his particular sect contains the whole truth of Christ."

"Yes; and they all prevail, according to their genius and character, as modified by Christ's words."

"Not, then, by the living Spirit of Christ?"

"No, not so much; for they have not, owing to the strife and division amongst them, succeeded in finding the perfect coat,—the true language which expresses the whole gospel truth. Controversy is the casting of the lots; and, in view of the wrong which this method of gambling has entailed upon the race, it is not hard to see that there is not a great gulf betwixt the swells of the world and those of the church."

"For shame, Malcolm! how dare you insinuate that clergymen, the only moral teachers we have, are no better than the fiends, who, having crucified the Lord, gambled and fought for his clothes?"

"Excuse me, friend, if I am too severe; but violent diseases require violent cures. The dragon's teeth have been sown amongst us; and, as the French Revolutionists swallowed each other up, I suppose we must fight for Life Eternal at the expense of all that pertains to time and space. I aspire to live in and for the genius of the united humanities, and have no peace beyond the satisfaction I take in so doing. The individual mind perishes, and this I say in full view of that immortal sea which brought me hither."

"I do not quite understand you. Are you a stranded vessel, or one that is safely moored in the haven that is?"

"Neither; or rather I am infinitely more than both; but, unfortunately, I am not all that I am bound to be. Remember, if we commune concerning the mysteries, we must hold all things in solution, and reproduce them at will. As my friend Shaft says, God only exists for the regeneration or recreation of himself in every living creature."

"Then you aspire higher than to the possession of a single coat?"

"Here is where we must be cautious; for we approach the inscrutable Fountain of Life, and no human eye can see, nor tongue can tell, what the Spirit is; no, not one, even if all Science was converted into a single eyeball for the sake of beholding Him once. We must needs be silent before Him, for we stand in the mansion of God; and if we look around us we may behold the prophets and holy men of old,—see how the ghosts speed by."

"You are a confirmed infidel and a mystic, Malcolm. I thought, after so long a passage, you would land me somewhere; but I am nowhere."

"Well, I will sail back and see if I cannot show you where you are. Let us cast lots again. There! you draw the longest one, and take the prize. I wish you joy. Let me help you on with the whole gospel truth! Now, you see, if I am an infidel, it is because you, not I, have obtained the whole coat."

"You are veering round at last, I see," said Arthur, laughing. "But, since you need it more than I, take it yourself."

"Certainly: I accept it gladly, and will wear it as long as I can. But, joking aside, Arthur, you see that we all need symbols of our own; and, granted even that the church makes them to order, it is necessary that we see to our measurement. Thus my infidelity, if there be any infidelity about it, is unfaithfulness to the style or method of other men. I recognize no authority but conscience and reason, which, in reality, are one and the same thing. I fashion my language according to their dictates; and in so far as I do this I am true to the will of God and the good sense of all humanity. But if, on the other hand, I willfully ignore or pervert their language, or that of better men, I am worse than the basest. The question between me, a self-sufficing thinker, and you, a churchman, is the same question which will always exist between the *re*-former and the person to be *re*-formed or regenerated."

"But who regenerated you, Malcolm?"

"Myself; and I came more naked into the world than I did when I was an infant. Christianity acted as my nurse, and gave me my swaddling clothes; but now, as a growing person, I look around for a suitable dress."

"It seems to me," said Arthur, "that you ignore the breadth of the denominational cloth."

"By no means; but the material is too poor. But let us drop the figure, and use plain speech. The fact is, Arthur, I will not go to the Old and New Testament alone for stuff, but ransack the universe, pick up the steamers from the seas, unfix the stars, invert volcanoes, and play football with the planets. There is no use talking. We must move in concert with the Eternal, as it dances from world to world, or rides on the waves of the ages, or rushes in righteous indignation in the whirlwinds of battle and confusion. It is not only the calm and the meek, the piteous aspect of Omnipotent Grief, that claim our worship, but the tempest and the fire of Holiness and Virtue. Begone, ye parts and partialities! betake yourselves to the nothingness from which ye spring! I will have the whole or none; the blackness with the light, the grave with the gay, the empty vague with the all-in-all."

"But it seems to me, Malcolm, that you carry your principles to extremes. I cannot tolerate the self-sufficiency which inspires your utterance. It is not in harmony with the genius of Christianity, as I understand it, to use such wild and incomprehensible language. Now, as ideas, even the idea of tolerance itself, are necessarily intolerant and exclusive of all that which hinders their realization in the world without, I must logically reject your opinions as errors; or, in other words, as a sincere Christian, I neither can nor will suffer any individual to sow tares with the wheat of my religion."

"So you, even in this advanced period, would imprison your theological opponents?"

"Why not? All society acts on the principle of limiting the power of the false and the bad. The jail compels the thief to obey the moral mandates of the land. How much more desirable to imprison the loose thinkers who sow the seed of error and confusion, which, taking root in the minds of the ignorant, spoil them for life! What is religious truth for, if not to be applied to the betterment of mankind? And, since he who interferes with religous truth interferes with that betterment, shall he not be punished accordingly?"

"Yes, if we can; but we have advanced so far in liberality and toleration that we must sympathize with one another in our immoralities, winking at the peccadillos of society, except those of injured women and vulgar clowns."

"Your irony is not inapt, Malcolm; but, considering this lamentable state of affairs, would I not be justified in confining those who, in spite of their splendid opportunities, reject salvation through Christ?"

"Yes, if you are good and strong enough to lift and throw the first stone. You see, our thought changes every day; you will at least grant that you grow in grace."

. "Certainly."

"Supposing, then, that when you were thirty you were, like Paul, so strong in the orthodoxies of your nation, that, in justice to the cause of truth, you felt it a duty to hang a Unitarian, would you, ten years afterwards, if you happened to become a Unitarian, hang an Orthodox?"

"Certainly. There are only two religions, — the religion of indifferentism and that of proselytism. If I am Orthodox, or whatever I am, I will be it like a man, not as a mere player or *dilletante*."

"So you would actually insist, if you could, in this age of religious independence, on making others accept a final statement of religion?"

"Certainly. I will preach Christ to the last, and confine the heretic if I can."

" Even me ? "

" Even you," cried the youth, waxing enthusiastic in his turn. " Death to the infidel, to all who hinder me, in so far as I represent the Truth ! "

" Good for you, brother ! but, of course, you do not believe yourself totally depraved."

" I suppose I must allow that I, considered apart from the Truth, which I love to represent, am altogether wrong. Yes, Christ is the way, the truth, and the life ; and I, alas, am indeed nothing ! "

" Well, in this case, Arthur, you ought to begin the work of reform by the massacre of yourself ; for, being altogether nothing, you cannot hope to advance the interests of Christ ? "

" So I do," said the undaunted Arthur. " True philosophy must begin with self-sacrifice ; and it is simply on account of man's depravity that he must lose his life in this world, in order to save it in the next. The death of to day is the life of to-morrow.

" I like that, Arthur ; but your logic reduces you to self-immolation ; mine, to self-preservation."

" But why reverse the whole order of Christian poetry ? "

" Because it is wrong to admit that Christ, as God, died even for a day."

" It is plain, Malcolm, that we cannot sail together. Like Dean Swift, you have gone to sea in a tub ; your experience will not impress people with the safety of independent spirit navigation. I envy those people who can wind up the universe and put it under their pillow when they go to bed."

# V.

## THE LAPSE.

MALCOLM, tossed about as we have shown on the waves of theological thought, would not, perhaps, have enjoyed his schooling so much had it not been for the prospect of his marriage with Miss Crisp. And the longer he dwelt on the happiness in store for him, the more tempted was he to lay aside his heretical ideas, and cast anchor in the safe haven of his sect. This consideration operated on his radical feverishness with hydropathic efficacy, and he began to deliberate how to deport himself under his present trying circumstances. For he was a well-meaning lad, and did not relish the prospect of becoming untrue to himself. All that he had to do to obtain the approval of the Church and the world was to make himself a passable minister of the Gospel, according to the somewhat mixed yet tenderly orthodox ideas of his expected father-in-law; which task, the reader will readily surmise, was not above the native ability and resolute industry of the lad, even if he had not the good luck of being called to the profession by special request of the Deity. "I can easily understand," he said to himself, "how a consistent mystic like Shaft can accept the doctrines of the Church by giving them a significance which no church or sect has yet done. But, while I admire the ingenuity and lofty ambiguities of that gentleman, it is not for me to adopt his or any other person's thought to the suppression of my own. Yet, as things are as they are, and not that which they seem, what am I to do? It seems as easy for me to appropriate the mystic ideas of Shaft as the coarse oratory of Progressive Bungle and Buzz, or the spiritual plaintiveness of Lullaby, or even the languid notions of any of the current vulgarities called creeds. God, if I understand myself at all, has evidently predestined me for an actor; and, this being the case, why should not I rejoice in the broad platform offered me by the Independent Spirit Navigation Sect of this grand and enlightened republic, as an appropriate stage for the exhibition of my talents? What an admirable combination the united wits of the said clergymen in one person would make! But, confound the thing! I hate hypocrisy, and cannot make up my mind to put on so hideous a mask, or, indeed, in any case not to speak as I feel, or adopt any part in the Drama of Life to the exclusion of the one I am best fitted to play. If I die for it, I am forced to confess that this man, Infidel though he is, is more honest, and has more truth on his side, than at least one-half of the clergymen."

Here he lifted up a tract, written by the Reverend Horatio Seiber, the left-hand man of the Free Theological Association, and read, —

"In place of the doctrine that 'there is no other way' to be saved from sin than through the blood and merits of Jesus Christ, we teach that man can be saved from the consequences of sin only by avoiding a sinful course of life, and that he will be far more likely to do this by trying to improve his own blood and merits than by depending upon the blood and merits of anybody else."

"Now," he continued, "in view of the palpable truth thus crudely, yet nevertheless strongly stated, which has been sanctified by a life of unswerving industry and intense devotion to his highest ideas of mental freedom, how can I conscientiously refrain from proclaiming the Truth as I now see and realize it to be? And yet I am called upon in the name of God and duty to put myself in the background, and preach the mixed notions which are vulgarly called Christ, which, shortly stated, amount to this, — namely, that all mankind, being doomed and deadened by the fall of the first Adam, can now be saved from eternal torment only by the mystic efficacy of Jesus' blood, a remarkable prophet who lived some two thousand years ago. Now that this scheme of salvation may, as Shaft explained, be a grand and comprehensive allegory, originally based on the pure logic of Reason,* as that is manifested in the Oriental imagination, and that it thereby could only have secured and maintained its influence over the mind of mankind, I have not the smallest doubt. Yet, while I plainly see and allow for all this, and would gladly use this allegory to the extent of my ability, even as I would the gift of language, which, after all, is only a collection of little images or allegories, having their origin in the

* The word is here used in the deeper transcendental sense which it has according to Kant and others.

observation and experience of the Spirit, I have no right whatever to ascribe to it any dogmatic meaning, or to substitute either it or any other trope, parable, symbol, or allegory for the Living Truth which all kinds of religious language unite in expressing, — namely, the simple fact that any person can, if he will, become worthy of a mission equally noble, equally divine with that of any deified hero who ever blessed the race. But, alas! how am I to express this Truth in a worthy manner, and publish it as it must be done to those who need it?"

Here he caught a glimpse of the vast amount of trouble and pain he would have to endure in order to do it justice. And as he dwelt upon the vistas of the dark future suggested, he shrank back appalled at the task; for it might indeed involve, to begin with, the sacrifice of his intended bride. Then the modern Devil, or that part of him which haunts the secret places of the Church, interwove himself with his thought, and spoke: —

"Ay, what will she say, and her father? and pray what canst thou hope to gain by this remarkable confession of faith in thyself, as opposed to the fortified opinions and embattled prejudices, the living Gods of the bishops and the lords, the deacons and the dukes of the world? Dost thou not see that thine eager affirmation will pass for blasphemy, thy reasons for the ravings of a visionary possessed, and thy love for the restless malice of envy and discontent? This insensate devotion to the Truth will not only deprive thee of the woman thou lovest, but give her and her father and all thy friends needless distress. And the gleaming ocean of social pleasures — creole manners, bright eyes, sympathetic satins, entrancing silks — which surround thee on all sides, skirting the shores of thy being with graceful curves and pleasant spray, will sink far beneath thee, and thou wilt be left alone on the naked summit of Egotism, there to see and suffer the consequences of rebellion. And behold, Zeus shall direct his Strength and his Force to bind thee in adamantine bonds; and the fire of his wrath shall nail thee to the gray rock of neglect and despair; and thy great but impotent sympathy with those who bear the burdens of the world shall lie in thy bosom like a living coal. And thou shalt cry aloud in the anguish of thy heart; for the Christian Zeus shall rise against thee in all the majesty of his might. Yea, the Lord, who is Lord of hosts, will hold thee in derision; and the thunders of his wrath will fall upon thy head; and the scream of the eagle which shall come to prey upon thy bowels will drown the voice of thy anguish. Where, then, shall be the thought or the forethought which can free thee from the horrible fate thy mistaken philanthropy shall precipitate upon thee? Steal fire from Heaven, thou fool! wherefore not rest content with things as they now seem? for the new hopes thou wouldst give to others are blind and very vague; and the creative fire thou art about to steal shall only consume thine own soul in the heat of unrequited endeavor. Thus thy punishment shall be well deserved, and descend, also, upon all who receive the fatal gift from thy hand; for the Lord, the Zeus of the Christians, is a jealous God, and will in nowise suffer any infringement of his Church. Behold, then, in a little while thou shalt disappear from the earth, utterly crushed by his thunders."

Here Malcolm laughed wildly at the novelty of his thought; for it was full of ghastly satire. And so the negative came off the victor, having made the young minister *prudently* resolve to defer the expression of his own thought. Like many a sainted individual before him, he naturally thought that the best thing he could do was to be as good and sincere a Christian as the circumstances would allow.

Thus he became very guarded in the expression of what little thought he chose to utter, lest he should suffer from the further imputation of heresy. He now saw the necessity of making longer prayers, — thus demonstrating the solemn truth, "the farther from God, the more prayer," — and to the surprise of his classmates appeared to appreciate certain arguments about the miracles, to which heretofore he had been quite impervious; whereat his teachers talked ominously about the mystic operations of the Spirit, and were pleased to allow that there was after all considerable in the lad, and that no doubt he would in time become a popular minister. And so carried away was the youth by the brilliant future in store for him, and so alive was he to the perils of being anything but a Christian in the most approved sense of that ambiguous word, that he even wrote pious letters to his beloved, and, laying Æschylus and Plato on the shelf, plunged at once into the depths of Paley, Spurgeon, and Beecher.

# VI.

## A LETTER FROM JENNIE, OR THE TANGIBLE RESULT OF DESERVING PIETY.

WHAT of Miss Crisp all this time? How had she been advancing, and had the Rev. Dr. Pluffle fairly transfigured himself in her sight? This last letter of hers to Malcolm may throw as much light upon the matter as the reader may require.

BRAGVILLE, TUESDAY.

DEAREST MALCOLM,

As I was spending the day with Julia Flippert when that letter of yours came in which you spoke so lovingly of your Redeemer, I did not receive it until tea-time. As soon as I had read and re-read it, I ran to show it to papa, who was delighted with it. He said he had no idea that you were so capable, and, — only think, Malcolm, — if you could only express yourself a little more decidedly about the Lord, you would be fit for one of the first pulpits in Bragville. But, strange to say, dear Malcolm, although I was overjoyed to see your recognition of Christ's merits, I did not think the letter like yourself. I missed a nameless something, which made me sad.

Dr. Pluffle called at his usual hour, and papa, in the course of conversation, glowing at the recollection of some of your words, made me show the letter to him, saying, "What do you think of that, brother? The boy is sound as a dollar. I've often told you so, but you scarcely believed me." Dr. Pluffle read the letter, and, looking queer, replied, that, although the tone of the letter was healthy, you had something to learn yet, as there were a few ambiguities in it which indicated "a slight departure from the blessed letter of revelation." But papa only smiled satirically, asking what he could expect from a lad of your originality, and told him that he need not be so particular in these radical times, since even Drs. Buzz and Bungle were not so sound as he would like to see them.

I must say, Malcolm, that, while I rejoice to perceive that you come nearer the Truth of the creed I miss that simplicity of speech which I admired in you at first. I am afraid, after all, there is more sophistry in Divinity schools than is good for the sacred cause. Really, I cannot understand why so long a time is required for young men to learn to preach and pray what they are supposed to know, or have by heart, already,— namely, the "Spirit of Infinite Self-sacrifice," as old Dr. Seegood, my mother's minister, used to call it. But we poor girls, with our little heads, are not expected to understand the systematic Theology which is essential to young ministers' salvation. That, however, may be one of the mysteries of Religion which not even the wisest, in the plenitude of their powers, are permitted to solve. "Poor, weak human reason," is Pluffle's motto, and there is more truth than poetry in it. But never mind my impertinence, dear Malcolm: keep doing your best, as you used to tell me to.

We've had much company of late, and Julia Flippert has been helping me. She's splendid. By the way, here's a present for you from papa (check for five hundred dollars), and there is another (for the same amount) which I want you to invest for my benefit. Get me an India shawl like pattern,— small figures, mind. Little people are frights in big figures.

You have not seemed so happy of late. Let us know if you are at all out of sorts: I miss you. I amuse myself trying to find out the meaning of those stories in the Arabian Nights you called my attention to. I have succeeded with one,— the very last story in the book. The mountain where the speaking bird, the golden water, and the singing tree are to be found is the Hill of Christian Progress, which the soul must ascend to obtain those gifts of perfection, the reward of patient effort and toil. The distracting voices which try to make people look back are the countless temptations of life. We yield, and are, as the story describes, immediately turned into black stones. Remember Lot's wife. The talking bird is Wisdom, who is the slave of those who find her. The best man delights in being the servant of his race. The bird points to the golden water, as Christ points to the Living. The good princess, after blaming the bird as the cause of her misfortunes, was glad to do its bidding, and sprinkle with the precious waters the black stones that these enchanted beings might be restored to life and activity. And did the bird not succeed, by dint of matchless judgment and art, in clearing away the difficulties that had beset the family of her mistress? When people have done their duty they always feel like singing. How natural to make Heaven a house of Eternal Song! The singing tree must represent the joy of the soul on obtaining the other gifts of grace. Therefore, Christ is at once the Great Singer, the Prophet, and the God. How many black stones have been disenchanted by the sprinkling of his Living Waters,— the efficacy of his Golden Words!

Yes, indeed, Malcolm, I am truly glad to find that you have at last shown some resolution, and turned your back upon those misguided men who call themselves radicals. There is now nothing to hinder you from becoming a successful minister, a devoted sprinkler of the Living Waters of Christ's Wisdom, and attaining the possession of the Singing Tree. Earnestly trusting that you will persist in the course you have taken,— you see our whole future depends upon it,— I remain, dear Malcolm,

Your own     JENNIE.

"How good she is, and true, in spite of the nothingness around her!" exclaimed the youth as he picked up the bright checks, and regarded them in an indescribable manner. "She is like a fresh-culled pond-lily, in whose petals a few aphides still linger; but they are easily shaken off. Yet what shall I do with this money? Well, I suppose I must do as I am told. Little people are frights in big figures. What a queer world this is,—what with miracles, creeds, religious sensibilities personified, fine shawls, and all the other glories of civilization! And this money my Christmas present, the thirty pieces of silver which I receive in exchange for betraying myself into the hands of the Scribes and Pharisees. What a conversion! I, who felt myself beginning to be a Jesus, am in a fair way to become a Judas. I must congratulate the Church on her acquisition. But there is no visible cross, so I will be saved the remorse of beholding the murder of my Master. Am I to be, or am I not to be? that is the ever-recurring question of the soul. And I reply in the negative. For there is no Truth, no God; and the man of Abstract Virtue is a fool, all language a fraud ; and there is no being worthy of regard save Force, whose very life is pleasure. He, then, shall be the God of my worship, and death to the vague botheration I loved to call my true self. So Force becomes my '*Etre Suprême*,' and I will be a Robespierre to the conscience which interferes with my joy. If the so-called life of zealous Virtue is the only real life, and that of obvious pleasure and respectable content mere sleep, I prefer to sleep on, even at the risk of doom. What am I saying? There is no doom for the strong man whose stomach is superior to his soul,—naught but ease, affluence, peace, joy, and good repute. What, pray, is Shaft compared with Crisp? The one twists the actual world into any shape he pleases, while the other makes a rope of sand or blows word-bubbles. What a fool I were to choose the lot of the latter! No! The man of matter, the owner of ships, stocks, pews, and all manner of stuff, is the living person, and the vague twister of words is the ghost. But this is rather a forbidding way of looking at it. Moderation in all things. I will be meek and mild with my '*Etre Supreme*,' oh, so meek and poor in Spirit, that I shall at once inherit the earth and the kingdom of Crisp's Heaven. For I will occupy a high place both in and out of the Church, and no man, in view of my son-in-lawship, and the pulpit I shall occupy, will dare say a word against me. And I will be liberal, so optimistically indulgent to other men's creeds, that I will pass for one of the best hearts in the country. But in this sleep of death visions may come. What if they do? I will make the most of them for the good of my kind. But the vision of the Eternal may come, even as it came before? Let it come: I will sleep on; and with the Church for a bed-fellow why should I care about the future? And her to whom you have given your truest love, will you be content to let her and her children sleep this sleep of death with you? Yes: for I am her Samson, and, Delilah-like, she has cut off my hair whilst I slept. But Samson knew not of his loss, and you willingly, gladly, endure yours. Woe betide you, Malcolm, for the Philistines are cruel and strong, and your '*Etre Supreme*' shall lose his strength with you. Up then, sluggard! out of this baneful sleep, and fly from the arms of Delilah. Her fondness is a snare, her wealth a horrible delusion. Not a bit of it! She is no Delilah, but a dear good girl, a nice Christian girl,—a little worldly it is true, but that is natural enough considering her position. And I, what am I but a poor young man who ought to think himself a lucky dog — confound it, I do not like the language of the age. But what need I care? For a truth there is enjoyment in sleep, and I shall sleep on; for there is no awakening. The die is cast, and I am content not to be anything but an ordinary, good-natured, free and easy, respectable member of society, hoping and praying that all is for the best, no matter what turns up. Back then, Conscience, and get thee gone, O Reason, to the mystic depths from which ye sprang. God or no God, Fiend or no Fiend, I am bound to enjoy myself as a worthy vessel of the Church, and as becometh a pupil of Bungle and Buzz. Here's to thee, O Force!" and the lapsed soul drank to that Darkness whose other aspect is Pleasure without Virtue.

Malcolm, strange to say, was logical and straightforward in his villainy. He did not cheat himself with the thought that he could make a pleasure of Virtue. Pleasure and Virtue may indeed go hand in hand for a brief moment now and then, but there are fatal obstacles to lasting peace between the two. And no doubt when the Lord refused to turn stones (words) into bread, and to fall down and worship his own Devil, he felt this to be true. Herein lies the strength of the position occupied by Jesus as the legal God of Christendom; for he is thought never to have fallen.

# VII.

## THE SPIRIT'S MEDIUM.

MALCOLM had not been long in Huberton before he became acquainted with an extremely well-meaning, yet rather bigoted clergyman, called Singleface, the father of the James who informed the faculty of his heresy. That gentleman, though at first repelled by the free humor of Lawson, soon perceived that he was as earnest at heart as he was light in his manners; and latterly, especially since the youth appeared to grow conservative, he took quite an interest in him, and ran the risk of inviting him to tea. For Brother Singleface, notwithstanding his intelligence, was no friend to those who reject the fixed doctrines of the Church. Yet he hated controversy, declaring that Religion was to be had and cherished as the best gift of God, and that the most absurd thing one could do was to attempt its defense. "For Religion," said he, "is life itself, or indeed that life in God into which no earthliness can come."

But, alas! this good old gentleman, whom all his acquaintances loved as their best friend, fell ill, and appeared to be on the point of death. Evidently he was not destined to survive his experience of the woful decadence of faith which attended the advent of the Rainbow Creed.

Malcolm called to see him during his illness, and had many edifying talks with him; for the near prospect of death is ever a stimulus to genuine thought. The sympathy and magnetism of the young man blended with the serene fervor and fixed piety of the old man, and the most perfect harmony subsisted between them.

"How," asked Malcolm one evening, "did you work among the poor without constantly bringing forward the letter of your creed?"

"The nature of my work was such that I did not even know that I had a creed. I relied on the Spirit, and he never failed me."

"Did you always feel so?"

"No," sighed the old man: "I have made many mistakes in this life. But the worst I ever made was compelling my children to believe precisely as I did. In my anxiety for their welfare, I think I was a little too strict with them, and I did not make the Truth so agreeable as I wished. My aim was to give them a deep love and reverence for the Word. But, alas! the Power of Darkness is very strong, and we are all so weak. What with our imagined progression, and theological eclecticism, dishonest politicians, and corrupt legislation, I fear we are on the high road to perdition. At a very early age my son proved unfaithful to my precepts, and only by a special intervention of Providence was he saved."

"Why! don't you approve of the liberal preaching of Drs. Buzz and Bungle?"

"No, not at all. Be warned by me, and as you

value your soul shun it as you would immediate ruin. The duty of the preacher is not to preach for the amusement of the vulgar, but to diffuse, by his own example, like the prophets of old, the principles of morality and practical religion. Not to discuss or to theorize about those principles; for that savors of all that is unwholesome. The well man speaks not of his health."

"But what shall we talk about?"

"Do not concern yourself about that. Give yourself up to the Holy Spirit, and then shall you ever say the right word."

"But," asked Malcolm, "don't the vulgar revivalist give himself up to him?"

"Alas! Malcolm, do not recall the revolting fanaticism which usurps the throne of the true Christian. Satan can quote scripture as easily as good angels."

"Yet how am I to treat these people?"

"Like the faithful doctor who will not leave his plague-stricken patients. The Holy Spirit is obedient to the will."

"How about Reason, in Kant's sense of the word?"

"The Spirit is always reasonable. There can be no conflict between Him and Reason."

"In this case, then, there is no difference between you and me. For Reason and Spirit are one."

"Surely, for the Reason is the right use of the faculties, as directed by the Holy Spirit, who responds to the prayer of the will."

"This, also, being allowed, Mr. Singleface, why

should honest Infidels and superstitious Christians consider themselves so far apart from one another? The Infidel believes in Reason to the exclusion of the thought of the Holy Spirit, while the Christian believes in the latter to the exclusion of the former. So, if Highest Reason and the Holy Spirit are one, both Christian and Infidel are essentially correct, in so far as each is faithful to his thought."

"Your argument is ingenious. I suppose I must agree with you."

"Well," said Malcolm, "let us exchange for a few days: you take the Holy Reason and use it, while I take in exchange the Holy Spirit, and use it to advocate the cause of essential religion, which is possessed alike by Jew and Gentile, Christian and Mohammedan."

"Tut, tut, my young friend. You are going too far. We must not forget the mystic efficacy of the Blood. But here comes that man Tightcreed. I know his step. Retire to the next room, and leave the door ajar."

As Malcolm retired, the said doctor came in.

The fact was that Drs. Tightcreed and Bungle, Lullaby and Buzz, thought it a duty, for the sake of appearance at least, to pay their departing friend, who was the most active person in the ministry, a farewell visit. The dying man, who was not very fond of these clergymen, hardly expected this ebullition of sympathy on their part; and, if he had not known them of old, he might have considered it a sign of reformation. At all events, he prepared to accept the condolence of each as he arrived, and to respond graciously to their considerate prayers for his recovery.

Tightcreed was the first to call, bringing a second-hand copy of the Doré Bible, a new treatise on the miracles, and sundry original tracts on the future life according to the consolatory and tempting views of his warmest friends in the Faith.

"These small tokens," said Tightcreed, sitting down, and laying the offering on the table, "testify to the appreciation the Christian world has for your devoted service in the Lord's cause. Take them, my dear friend, and may the comfort you derive from their perusal lighten your heart; and if they do not ensure a return to health, they may assist you to cross the dark river which divides you from the glorious beyond. For hopeful, ever hopeful, is the Word, — ay, beyond all conception, hopeful and precious is the Word. Trust it now, trust in it ever as ye have heretofore done; and through this trust, as evinced in resignation to His will, you will secure a harp and a crown in the house of the blessed."

Here Tightcreed, whose red nose shone approvingly on a bottle of spirits which raised its attractive stopper high above the Doré Bible, as if quite displeased at the intrusion of its deadly enemy, paused for an answer.

Mr. Singleface, however, took no notice of Dr. Tightcreed's benignant regards on the spirits, and replied, "Many thanks, worthy friend, for all your care and attention. I will look at your gifts with pleasure; but before I go to my Father let me speak one word of advice. May I speak as the Spirit moveth me?"

"Surely, surely, my good friend, say what you please; for there is wisdom in the words of the departing."

"Well, then, Dr. Benjamin Tightcreed, even while I appreciate your kindness in thus coming to see me, I regret being obliged to charge you with abuse of the Spirit."

"What!" exclaimed the doctor in a great rage, "have I come here to be insulted?"

"Pardon me," said the dying man, with a look of such deep melancholy that Dr. Tightcreed was taken aback. "Man is a poor weak creature, yet the Spirit is omnipotent. O my friend, in your vain attempts to make the letter alive ye have killed your soul. Mark well my words; for they are my last to you. Yes, your creed has strangled the Spirit. And I see it now for the first time. Good God! how does it happen that my whole thought is changing? No: it cannot be I that am speaking. But leave me, Tightcreed, — away and repent." (The Spirit had entered him.)

That gentleman was indignant; but, putting on a look of pity, he said, "Good-by, my poor friend. Let me call the doctor on the way." He then left, muttering, "His mind has left him quite."

No sooner had he retired than Dr. Progressive Bungle came in, bringing a large basket of flowers, some fine jelly of all colors, and a few cream-cakes. "Ah, my dear Singleface, I am truly sorry to see you, the active soul of our denomination, so low.

But cheer up, old heart, there is a glorious future in store for us. There are four rainbows in the sky,— the four great hopes of immortality. Yet how fleeting the life of man! What difference does it make, after all, whether we remain here a day or two longer in this contemptible garb? For my part"—

"Stop, friend!" cried Singleface, with a savage brightness in his eye: "do you refer to the flesh, or to the cloth?"

Here Progressive Bungle laughed heartily; for he enjoyed nothing more than a joke, and was rather noted for his "slants at theologians." "Jokes," he used to say, "are plums in the Bread of Life, whose butter is unction." But his enemies maintained that his Bread of Life was served too hot and fresh to answer their digestion.

"Upon my word," he replied to Mr. Singleface, "that is as good a thing as I have heard for some time past. But you are unusually severe. What's up? The fact is, a man in my position is different from anybody else. I never was called to the work with you. And I often wish that I had not been forced into this uncomfortable position which hinders me from doing and saying what I please. However, since we must allow that all things are for the best, why should we who love the Lord concern ourselves about this empty world?"

"Speak, Bungle, for yourself. I am willing to die for your sake, if need be, for I love you. But you, alas! I feel in my heart, have little or no love for me. The spectacle of thy theological looseness has cut me to the core."

"My poor friend," replied Bungle, with a concerned air, "has the doctor been here this morning? I have no doubt but you will recover soon, when we will be as good friends as ever."

No sooner had he left the room than in walked Dr. Lullaby, with a new edition of fashionable hymns in his hand, and an illustrated volume of Tennyson's "In Memoriam," which he gave him, saying, "My dear Bostonio (this was Mr. Singleface's first name), I was much grieved to hear of your sickness, and I come on the raven wings of sympathy, with a tender bit of Life's Bread in my hand. Let me read my favorite verse, —

> "'Ring in the valiant man and free,
> The larger heart, the kindlier hand;
> Ring out the darkness of the land,
> Ring in the Christ that is to be.'

"I have no doubt but an occasional look at those poems will have a favorable effect on your constitution. Why should you leave us so soon? Lay aside all thought of the grave, and enjoy the hour that is. For, believe me, my dear friend, there is nothing to be gained by dwelling morbidly upon our common lot. Just see the sun. How beneficently he shines upon us all! And, hark! hear the joyful song of the birds, and the rare touch of the nimble-fingered wind as he playfully attempts the accompaniment on the trees. Forget your grief. All will yet be well with you."

"But not with you, friend Lullaby," cried the savage old man; "for you — yes, you, Doctor Simon

Lullaby — will go to Hell. For thou art the fiend who hast done more to put me on my death-bed than any other individual. Thy seductive soothing has lulled to destruction a thousand souls, who, had they been faithfully spoken to, might each have been a Hercules. Dost thou think that He, if he were here in view of the fraud and corruption of the times, would preach as thou dost? Get thee gone, old Half-and-Half! I'll none of thee. No wonder infidelity to common honesty rears his kelpy head high above the fountains of the churches to swallow up the young of Christianity."

"The man is mad," cried Dr. Lullaby, thoroughly alarmed. "Let me run for the doctor;" and he rushed from the room.

Scarce had the door closed behind him, which it did with a bang, when Oratone Buzz appeared, with the solemn yet easy air peculiar to the ecclesiastical beau, carrying a basketful of sea-shells from the Isle of Shoals and a bag of game from the Adirondacks; for he was both a yachtsman and a man mighty in the hunt.

"My dearest friend," he began, "I" —

"Excuse me sir," cried the old man, who was perfectly frantic at sight of the game. "I am not your dearest friend. Do you think the dollars and cents your dulcet tones have wrung from the pockets of doubtful characters, from Mr. Twentypercent and Mr. Bad Guttapercha, will mend the souls of the poor, when you cannot begin to mend either your own or those of your fashionable pew-holders? I'll none of your sea shells, I'll none of your game;

for they are bought with coin of Hypocrisy and Deceit. Leave me, if ye have the least regard for my health."

Here Oratone fled from the room, realizing for the first time that his deacons might have read the Bible to better advantage than he.

Then Malcolm came from out the next room, and, falling on his knees beside his friend's couch, cried in a loud voice, "O Heaven, help me to be faithful to the Truth as I now see it through the dying words of my friend! of him who, while I was faint for the want of strength, gave it me when I least expected it! And may I never again fall from the high place I have chosen! from which the cities of men, great though they are, seem but grains of fertilizing salt on the field of the soul!"

He then looked up, but, lo! the old man was fast asleep; as yet there was no corpse.

"Surely," cried the youth, "the old man must be a splendid medium. I will do what I can for him. I will take good care of him, and, after all, the doctors have left considerable life in him. He improves."

Thus Malcolm — who, by the way, had not been able to become so bad as he had tried to be — recovered his footing, and henceforth resolved to keep himself upright. He went home determined to write no more loving letters about his Redeemer.

The Word that was Light still shines, but, alas! the darkness has gathered: yet, behold! in the far west a gleam of glory is seen. What can the shower of falling drops but restore to the sun the imperfect reflex of his own face!

# VIII.

## SELF-RELIANCE.

EARNEST endeavor to do right, to make the most of ourselves, is, to say the least, a notable thing; and, if we properly respect it, it is astonishing to find with how much of the so-called supernatural we can dispense.

Malcolm, under his present circumstances, entangled as he is in the meshes of infidelity to infidelity, is not unlike the fox that, being caught in a trap, could only extricate itself at the expense of its tail. What a painful experience for the poor fox! what an admirable illustration of the necessity of self-reliance! But the end of this fable amused us more than the beginning. The tailless fox went and told his brethren that it was, upon the whole, much better to be without the bushy appendage, and kindly advised them to go and do likewise. But they could not "see it." Nor can we blame them. Thus it is with the Godless and the Godful; both try to make proselytes.

Why this endless discussion about the simple fact of God? Does the Divine Idea not grow with those who conceive it? How the gods of the Christians change! The last judgment has lost its terrors, and the bland idols of progressive preachers offer a hell-less future to a callous world.

Malcolm's superstitions and worldly prospects were to him what the tail was to the fox. If thy right hand, or even thy right eye, offend thee (mortifies), get rid of it; for it is better that it should perish than thou thyself.

In this connection, being led into unexpected depths, we feel called upon, not merely to moralize, but even to sermonize, in the midst of our story. Hear the following extract from a lecture by Mr. Shaft:—

"Temptation! what is this most mystic experience of the soul? A person is offered an obvious and palpable benefit,— it may be a jeweled crown or even a fair woman's love, — yet, in spite of the ambition boiling within him like an imprisoned volcano, or in spite of the grasping tentacles of hungry desire (Dêvil-fish), he disdains the offer. 'What a morbid fool!' cries one; 'he fears the pains of Hell, and with praiseworthy and Christian caution refuses to peril his soul.' But suppose that his fear is only that of ordinary white-faced Death, with a star of flowers on his breast, asleep on the cold couch of nonentity, or rather that he has no fear at all, but either rests on the firm conviction, or somewhat faint-heartedly believes that that alone which he feels to be right is the proper thing to be done. But look, brethren, as ye will at this experience of yours, you will find something in it which mocks the power of words. Nor Moses, nor Elijah, nor Daniel, nor Shadrach and his companions, concerned themselves about their future lives, yet they preferred deserts, a lion's den, and a fiery furnace to all that Pharoah, Ahab, and Nebuchadnezzar had to bestow. Thus the holy man, or the person who is wholly of God, stoops not to weigh the results of his manliness, but is, on the other hand, so superior to those deeds which his inferiors call miracles, that he speeds onward like the sun-god, unconscious of doing aught remarkable. What fearful fate is this which, in the midst of enlightenment and evolution attained, makes people a prey to the most despicable tempters. The progressive individualist claims to have advanced beyond Christianity. Is he quite sure that he is up to the laws of Moses? Yet have a care, O World, concerning those progressive or anti-progressive citizens of thine. There may be, for aught thou knowest, prophets amongst them great even as those of ancient time, or there may be mad conspirators beneath thy splendid cities piling up kegs of the same nitro-glycerine which tore Paris in pieces. But, not to speak of trying to distinguish between these friends and foes of thy household, it might be well to ascertain whether there is any difference between him who is infidel to thy idols for the sake of being true to his own God, and him who is false to conscience for the pleasure of being true to thee and thy golden images. Methinks the spectacle of 'Him crucified,' wing~d by a couple of malefactors, were lesson enough. And it were well to remember that, how great soever the person who comes to thee laden with his Father's wealth, his life, to use St. John's words, is the light of men, not the substance of them; for are we not all, being made in God's image, possessed of the majesty of self-hood in some other sense than coin from the mint? What if we ourselves were gods, and our earthly existence only one of our dreams or nightmares? Enoch, Moses, Elijah, Jesus, it is said, left no remains behind them. They must have gone back to Heaven in the fiery chariots of their own bodies, the material of their dreams. 'None of your stuff,' says the wise man. Does he strike at the idealist or the materialist? The dictionaries, I notice, have no compliments to spare for that word. Strange, that those who pride themselves on their matter should have no regard for their stuff."

## IX.

### THE ORIGIN OF A PUBLIC INSTRUCTOR.

MR. SINGLEFACE naturally idolized his two remaining children, a boy and a girl, and gave great attention to their spiritual education. But here the bias of his mind, his absorbing, yet one-sided, devotion to the Great Invisible, interfered with their welfare and his own happiness. In his treatment of them he resembled the King in Æsop's fable, who, dreaming that his son would be killed by a lion, confined him in a lonely tower for safe-keeping, to the verification of his dream. Dread of the perishable was his dream, and his Creed the supposed tower of safety. A zealot himself, this gentleman labored to make zealots of his children, while they, either by reason of different mental constitution, or that peculiar perversity so often found in the families of the pious, did not appreciate the care lavished upon them, although, at the same time, they did not appear to think their instruction untrue. Their youthful minds, taught from infancy to regard the smallest doubt as a suggestion from Satan, were easily led into thoughtless acceptance of Christian doctrine, even while their sensuous instincts, unoccupied by the exercise of Reason, rebelled against it, manifesting their sedition in stolen self-indulgence. And so occupied was the parent in advocating Redemption by supernal self-sacrifice that he saw not the redeeming influence of simple Thought. Alas! society constantly repeats the experience of the daw who stole the peacock's feathers. Instead of so living that we, like all genuine prophets, may speak, as if inspired by God, we lead mean lives, and adorn our inferior thought with their sublime language, the cast-off clothing of superior ideas.

Mr. Singleface, it would seem, was born a century too late; for he acted on a stage quite unsuited to his merits. In vain he elevated the banner of his humble faith, and energetically used the old-fashioned sword of the Spirit in defense of his well-beloved cause. People did not care to follow him, and, attracted by the flowing banners and brilliant weapons of the Buzzes and Lullabys, left him for them. Therefore, as years flew by, he had to withdraw from the front rank of the Lord's army, and, falling into the rear, occupied himself with the care of the wounded. He now subsisted on his earnings as a city missionary. His family attended the church of Dr. Lullaby, whose marvelous creed, like the pair of seven-league boots in the fairy tale, — they fitted giants as well as Tom Thumbs, — was adapted to the spiritual dimensions of all Christians. And perhaps the manner and the character of the teaching, James and Mary Singleface — for so they were named — received from that Knight, in addition to their innate predisposition to error, prevented them from becoming so good as their father labored to make them. But be this as it may, both began, — especially James, — at an early age, to deceive him, and continued to do so even after they had become proficient in biblical literature. And they found it an easy task; for Mr. Singleface's eyes, being ever fixed on the stars of his Religion, could not see the weeds which were robbing his flowers of nourishment. "Duty, duty, my son; prayer, prayer to the Most High," he would say to the young man, while the latter, pious for the moment, would assent, or heave a sympathetic sigh, to keep, as he told a companion, the old man in heart, and then go off on a spree.

It is indeed no pleasant task to use the dissecting knife on so delicate a subject as this, but, as our vision has been greeted with so much disorder of the kind mentioned, we think it a duty to draw attention to it, leaving the application of Remedy to the Reason of those concerned. Blind Belief has proved itself quite incompetent.

Mr. Singleface's pet desire had been to educate his son for the Church; but of late years the conduct of that youth had been such that he almost despaired of his being fit for that noble calling. Two years ago James was found, by a policeman, in one of the vilest haunts in the city, and brought home intoxicated. What a blow to the innocent old man, — all his tender solicitude, his tearful anxiety and prayer thus set at naught! In the depth of his grief he wished that his son never had been born. Heart-broken, he sought the presence of God, and there found hope and consolation again.

Mr. Singleface saw at last that he had been a little too strict with James. He relaxed his exhortations. But it was too late. Even into the tower of his creed, the lion had penetrated. He had so worried him about his soul that the boy often wished he never had so inconvenient an appendage, and hated all that reminded him of it. The gloom of his home drove him to seek brightness elsewhere, and, being taught to think all the world was bad, he could not discriminate between the false and the true. Plants brought up in the shade must not be thoughtlessly exposed to the sun.

James was a good-looking, slender youth of twenty-one at this time. All danger of an early death from his hereditary complaint seemed past.

Young Singleface could not but be moved by the sorrow he caused his father and his sister. He vowed repentance, and henceforward did behave himself better. It could not be expected that a weak son of Adam would give up his bad habits all at once. We must have indulgence for "miserable sinners." At least, so thought old Mr. Singleface, who was busy thanking his God for the improvement visible in the boy, and praying with renewed vigor that he might become fit for the sacred cloth.

A sensible man might have seen at a glance that James was not fit to become a public instructor. But the mind of ignorant piety has so much faith in its gods, and so little, or indeed so much, in human nature, that it believes that the most depraved, with the aid of the Holy Spirit, may become at a moment's warning reliable preachers of what they call the Gospel.

Not long ago the wickedest man in Gotham held prayer meetings in his tavern. We cannot say whether he ever brought any souls to Christ, but we know that he brought many to himself. It is quite common to meet with young men in the country who unite some profitable employment with preaching salvation, such as the selling of maps, razors, prayer-books, small tooth combs, and the latest quack medicine. We never could tell whether the preaching was to assist in the sale of their wares, or their wares in the sale of the preaching. We guess that the latter must be the correct view, as we are bribed by chromos to subscribe to the *oldest* and *newest* of religious magazines. We make this digression to illustrate the power of the spirit as manifest in the turning of indifferently pious characters into devotees of art and manufacture, and *vice versa*. Jesus drove the money-changers from the temple. There is now worse than money-changing in that place. Who will drive it out?

Mr. Singleface was never tired of exhorting his son to give up all, and follow the Lord with the pastor's crook in his hand.

Now James Singleface was not altogether a fool, nor was he a hardened reprobate. He was simply an ordinary young man, who loved a good time, and was not particular how he got it.

He had been looking about him of late, and observing what a free-and-easy time such as Oratone Buzz and Dr. Lullaby were having: the truth suddenly dawned upon him that the "crook" was not such a contemptible thing.

"I wonder if I have a good voice," was the inspiration of the moment: "why can't I turn Deuteronomy and Lazarus to some account?" How natural for such a youth in his circumstances to speak thus! His father was poor, his own living was bad, and his business prospects were inferior. Would it not be a good thing for him? As a simple shepherd of the Lullaby school, he would not have to work so hard, and with the crook in his hand he could sing sweetly to a fashionable flock, and be well remunerated for his trouble. He blamed himself for not seeing it before.

"By Jove!" he exclaimed one day to a companion at the bar, — the tavern bar, — "the old man wants me to enter the Vineyard of the Lord. What do you say to it, William?"

William was one of those fat, indolent, lethargic customers who, if they be only vouchsafed cigars, lager beer, "The Huberton Herald," and enough scrip in their wallets to pay their week's board, are content to dream or babble away their existence in a saloon, only awakening to a sense of realities on election days, or at a call from the bar-tender to participate in that delectable Yankee entertainment called "poultry raffling," or on a notice to quit from a landlady whose creed is not favorable to late hours. In answer to James' question, William began by discharging a volume of smoke, and, looking up, seemed lost in thought for a moment. Then, giving his head an astute turn to one side, he looked at his friend, and laconically said, "You might do worse."

"I'm blessed if I mightn't," was the hasty reply of the impulsive James. "But, confound the thing, I ain't pious enough!"

"It will come," said the sententious William, with a glance that indicated a vast fund of inward conviction, which he valued so highly that he seemed desirous of keeping it all to himself.

"How the deuce will it come?" inquired the youth, taking the remnant of his cigar out of his mouth, and flinging it upon the saw-dust covered floor. "I don't see my way very clearly."

"Go to Jesus and cultivate your voice," was the dry response, delivered with mock gravity. "If I didn't sta-m-m-er, I would have been in the ministry long ago."

James had no difficulty in understanding William. He had often deceived his father and he could easily deceive the public also. But did his conscience not tell him that he was about to make a whited sepulchre of himself? It did and it did not. How could his reason or other gift of insight penetrate the obscurity of the superstition in which he had been brought up! He knew it was wrong to lie. But he did not see that he was going to lie. He coaxed himself into the belief that he was, as he termed it, *going in* for Christian truth. "I am indeed," he felt, "rather a tough candidate for the cloth, but are we not all miserable sinners? I do not know that I am any worse than the rest of them. In entering the ministry I only do the best I can for the Lord and myself. Religion is not hard to be got. I have often felt a mysterious alloverishness within me, exhorting me to rise and proclaim aloud the praise of my Maker."

He acquainted his father with his resolution. The old gentleman was delighted with this unexpected intelligence. He felt it to be a special interposition of the Almighty in his favor. He had no idea how much lethargic William, and other little secularities of his son had to do with it.

James had been in the college for some time before Malcolm came to it. At first he was not very favorably received on account of the little looseness that still clung to him. But latterly it was different, and the Faculty appeared to think that the apostolic mantle of his father was about to descend upon his shoulders. What splendid essays he wrote on the miracles, Peter, Paul, and the beauty of his Redeemer's character!

However, notwithstanding his natural abilities and the pious tone of his discourse, he continued to evince a fondness for lethargic William and the genial pursuits of that citizen. He paid him many surreptitious visits.

Yet, so struck were Tightcreed, Lullaby, and Buzz with the beauty of his prayers, and the elegance of his speech about his dear Saviour, that he was among the first to participate in the delights of preaching in this benighted or enlightened (whichever you please) portion of the globe at so much a Sunday.

Here is an instance of the character of James, to show how little pious words have to do with genuine fervor of soul. He invited several students into his room to hear him read an essay on Marcus Aurelius. While some looked over his shoulders, and others lounged about the room, he sat at the window and read the product of his labor in unctuous tones. He had come to the end of this passage, which we quote verbatim: —

"With what distress of soul, dearly beloved brethren, we regard the fact that Marcus Aurelius, in full view of the heroism evinced by the Christian martyrs, notwithstanding the many opportunities he had of embracing the truth of Christ, and thus earning himself a seat before the throne of Heaven, remained to the end of his days a cold, callous" —

Just at this moment a pretty girl passed the window and stopped on the sidewalk evidently to wait for the horse-cars. James Singleface's falcon eye saw her, and, stopping short, he cried out, "Quick, boys, Brown, Jones, here! quick! Look at that pretty girl, ain't she a beauty?" Marcus was forgotten at once, and five heads were instantaneously congregated in the window, where they contemplated with the most orthodox delight the said phenomenon. In five minutes James returned to his essay, and, resuming the pious tone, finished the period with the word "philosopher." It was pretty evident that he did not intend to remain to the end of his days a "cold, callous philosopher." His Christianity would not admit of such heathenism.

# X.

## THREE DOLLARS AND COSTS.

WERE you ever in a public court? There is where we first saw astute, lethargic William. He was fined three dollars and costs, as were a host of others. Three dollars and costs, — and costs, — how dolefully these words reverberate in our minds, and, like the presence of the spectre at the feast, quell the mirth that ought to reign over the board!

Alas William, thou art not the only sufferer. Avert thy wrath from the scowling, or as it may be jocular, justice, *pro tempore*, and visit it elsewhere. Canst thou count? Yes. Well, count the cost of thy act of intemperance. Canst thou not, by any stretch of imagination, get beyond the lucre to cost of another kind? William, thou hast sowed the wind and art a raiser of whirlwinds which the whole world must help thee to reap, for humanity is one and has a common barn for the storing of woe as well as of weal. How true thy slang, "to raise the wind," and thou art but one of the humblest sowers of that terrible seed!

Therefore the actual costs of our vices are the plagues that turn our common weal, even as they turned Egypt's, into common woe; and yet we chuckle if we are only mulcted in the costs, and triumphantly jingle the saved coin in our pockets.

What turned our Southern rivers into blood, and peopled the Southern plains with skeletons? What brought the frog-like shoddies, the swarms of fly and centipede-like quacks, the locust-like hypocrites to prey upon our greenness and our sweetness? Nor is the darkness gone, nor has Azrael ceased to rob us of our first-born and of our second, and yet, in full view of this terrible growth of Death, whose every leaf is a pestilence, we become bereft of wonder and merely sigh as the apples thereof fall in the midst of the community. Three dollars and infinite woe. We tell thee, O William, and all you that premeditate an act of vice, however insignificant it may seem to you, that the consequential damages are worthy of note. Therefore withhold your anger from the external inflicter of distress, and hoard it for another, whom neither Oratone Buzz nor Dr. Lullaby can appease, — namely, your own evil propensities.

This world of ours is an enchanted palace, and we are all half marble and half men, like the King of the Black Isles, in the Arabian tale. But are we all worthy of being compared with that dignified monarch?

We have often seen men that resembled wheelbarrows, and not respectable, sound wheelbarrows either, but very inferior ones with the wheels askew. Did you never see one of those vehicles asleep, upright on its shafts under the lee of a barn, without being reminded of a fop in a frock coat leaning against a lamp post in a fit of drunken inanition? His is a terrible fate. How can he return to his vileness, warned against it as he is. But what is the use of preaching, if the conscience of the community is debauched? A hypocrite — the greatest of all — is unmasked, but this, far from taking away his popularity, doubles it at once. But the severity of the law continues to those who have neither wealth nor fame nor eloquence to gild their sinfulness. Is this answer to charges of social delinquency not justified by living examples? "I am stronger than the Truth. The whole republic will gather itself together at my command, and roll itself like the deluge upon you. Do you think it will see me, its guide in war, its prophet in peace, the pride of its religion, perish like an ordinary minister of the gospel? No! Even as the northern lights shine night after night, crowning the mountains with magnificence, I shall stand inaccessible to reproach. The nation is mine, and I will pit its vulgar omnipotence against your spiteful truthfulness; and even if my heart should be spiked again and again, and in its agony burst open, I will endure unto the end; for in spite of all my naughtiness, I am one of those little children to whom the kingdom is revealed."

Strain away, O Public, at your gnats, and swallow your camels till you have had your fill. If the hated Paris of the South should suffer woe unutterable for meddling with the dusky Helen of King Sambo, what shall be done to him of the North who blackens the white wives of his neighbors? There are dead men's bones under that flaming crown of the frigid north, the aurora borealis. But a little more progressive bungling, and you will find the short cut to Paradise, the celebrated northwest passage, so necessary to spiritual commerce. But you need for the voyage a little more scrip than the Master recommends. Yet one of the said "little children" may lend you one of his fast horses or yachts to make the experiment,—he cares so little for the things of this world. But it may be objected by the religious, that the horse is a sacred animal, and that the ancient Egyptians were right in dedicating it to God; and that so fine a symbol of divinity ought not to be used as a beast of burden for ordinary men. Therefore, let there be high priests and imposing edifices in honor of its spiritual significance, for it is of the utmost importance to the human soul, in its present fallen condition, that it should become alive to God, as he is revealed in a magnificent stud. And in regard to yachts, oyster suppers, Burgundy, &c., would it not be a good thing to sanctify them unto the Lord, as peculiar institutions, predestined for the exclusive use of the high priests, as were of yore the tidbits of the sacrificial lambs, after Jehovah's nostrils had been duly gratified? In this case, then, we might be entertained with less scandal, and the first steps taken to inaugurate the millennium. If Mohammed went to heaven on an ass, why should we not be content with that mode of transit, and willingly accord to a popular progressive the privilege of a fast horse, and of such refreshment as would enable him to perform the extra duty of pioneer?

But count the costs, count the costs. We tried

to smile, but could not, when, a few days ago, we paid, in heavier coin than in that of the mint, a tax bill of another sort from that marked U.S. Our heads are very apt to be in moonshine while our feet, or what is worse, our hearts, are in very objectionable places. Mr. Singleface is not an isolated phenomenon. "But," one says, "I feel certain that I will escape the costs." We sincerely hope he will. An engineer said so, or something like it, before his native city followed the example of another, and burned itself to the ground. Let those that stand or sit, even as high as the chair of the great Continental Miracle Protection Association and speculate in gold and whiskies, take heed, for who knows what to-morrow may bring with its dawn. A friend of ours caught, during the night of the fire, a little boy in his bedroom setting fire to it. Probably he had sinned once himself, for he only thrust the incendiary out of doors. Who owns that boy, and who is there to shed a tear over him? The whole world is responsible for him and shall suffer from him, even as he who cleanseth not himself shall suffer from vermin.

What is going on in the vineyard of the Lord, or the nursery of the soul? We hear a song. Dr. Lullaby-by-by-by, Dr. Lullaby, thou rockest a tender baby in that cradle of thine. But what is that that I see? Serpents — spoon-headed, dragon-bellied, diamond-eyed, and with horrible fangs — quite close to its pillow. They are charmed and even sent asleep by thy splendid voice. Thou puttest forth thy hand as if to cut away their poison bags, when behold, they shake themselves, and heaps of golden scales cover the floor. Remember where thou art. Would that thy baby had the strength of the infant Hercules!

# XI.

## A RADICAL LOVE LETTER.

MALCOLM returned, as we said, to his room reproaching himself for his infidelity to the Truth, and firmly resolved to write no more loving epistles about his Redeemer.

What did he intend to do? He hardly knew himself. With his anti-traditional sentiments he could no longer accept the bounty of Mr. Crisp, nor hope that that miracle protector would rise above his prejudices and accept him for a son-in-law. And Jennie! To her whom he loved so well he would have to bid farewell, probably forever, as it would take him many years to work himself into a position that would enable him to support her. How would she take this change in his views, his resignation of the profession that was to constitute his claim to her hand!

He remembered how hard she had fought with her father in his behalf, how tender and true she was to him, notwithstanding her religious prepossessions (what could he expect from her age?), how all her little plans of future happiness were bound up with his well-doing; and he almost writhed in pain at the thought of offending her, of destroying the solid-looking air castles she had built for them both. She would never be able to understand his position or the true character of his resolution, as she had been brought up to believe even doubt of revelation a sin against the Holy Spirit. "A faithful infidel," said he: "but these words have puzzled wiser heads than hers. Yet I will write and learn." So he wrote:—

DEAREST JOY OF MY LIFE,—

Thou who art more to me than any earthly good, since I love thee with the Spirit I have from God, hear how I deceived thee for the convenience of the day, to the lasting perdition of us both. Verily, 'tis a hard task that I have chosen to confess myself thus; for I know not how I shall regain the place in thy esteem which this confession of mine may cause me to forfeit as just punishment for my sin. But even if I lose it and thee forever, I must be true to my best thought and purest aspiration to remove from my mind the burden of my guilt. Canst thou believe me, dearest, when I tell thee that I, Malcolm, whom thou hast chosen to complete the circle of thy life, have been for some time past a sorry fool and a conscious cheat? God, in a direct ray from himself, revealed to me the sacred duty of the hour, yet I turned away from the vision of glory and followed an evil of my own choice. Yes, voluntarily, and in the full knowledge that I was injuring myself and all those with whom I am connected, I pandered to a sensual superstition in that I pretended to believe a creed against which every fibre of my conscience rebelled. And this did I with that cowardice of soul which said, "Fear and tremble, evanescent spark of life inferior, for Force, in all his power and glory, is there; and, behold, in his right hand is Pleasure, and in his left Pain. Bow down before him, as the winds fan the knees of the mountains, and the mountains themselves bristle and cower in his presence, while the seas rise up in terror." And I did bow down before him and worship him according to his image, as graven in the books of the church. But now I repent and am glad; for I am myself again.

So much, then, dearest one, for the poetic view of my sin, — please to hear the prose. To lie was cheap and convenient: so much so, indeed, that, fearful of losing you, and dreading discovery more than death, I followed the example of Bungle and Buzz, and lied so well that men called me orthodox to the backbone. Or, in other words, to please the people, and particularly the faculty of the college, that I might as soon as possible enter the joy of their Lord, I sinned against my own Holy Spirit; for truly, up to the hour of my lapse, my purpose was pure and whole. Here you have the plain facts, and I have no excuse to offer, save the hope that I was not myself when I acted in this way; or the possibility that your fair image took on a false blazon, which so enchanted me that I could see no Divinity but itself. Now, had I loved you truly, this had not happened, and the apple remained uneaten. The first suggestion of Deceit that I yielded to robbed you of my love, and hid it in the house of Mammon. Your father, good, kind, charitable as he is, has built a high altar to his particular God; and I, with the vanity of my profession, looked forward with delight to the sinecure of high priest. But now, thank the realization of my folly as it is visible in others, my eyes are open, and I come again into harmony with a clear conscience and an upright understanding. A lie is a lie, no matter how brilliantly written or done, and it seemed to me yesterday, after sending you a Christmas gift, that, if I did not undeceive you, it was the same as if I had concealed a serpent in the case. I know it is false to suffer people to believe that the Scriptures were plenarily inspired; that Jesus, the son of Mary, was one with God in some peculiar mode of being unshared by others; that it is essential to salvation to believe the miracles and other traditions; that the Christian is the only mode of salvation capable of saving us from Eternal Punishment; and that Christianity and no other religion had its source in genuine revelation from God, &c. Therefore, even to retain your love and find everlasting favor in the sight of your father, I have no right to accept the articles of his creed and burn incense on the altars of his God; for my whole service belongs to Him who lives, moves, and has his being in all worthy persons as well as they in Him. Do not think that I, in such a Babel of theology and purblind dilettanteism as this, am weak enough to discuss the question of Jehovah or Christ or any other person who symbolizes in himself the Creator of the Universe. That, indeed, may not be below the dignity of the Bishops of world and the great editors of New Humbleton journals, but it certainly is infinitely beneath mine. So, as you see, I only protest against the degrading superstition and the altogether inadequate thought of both church and school, which hides from the people, in stereotyped forms and artificial speech, a greater knowledge of simple goodness. It is not the poor carpenter's son of Judea, who went about doing good in the most whole-souled manner, and with the most absorbing enthusiasm, but the Heir-apparent of the throne of Heaven, who condescended to share for a season the state of spirit incarnate, that compels their worship. But, whether I am right or wrong, in respect of theology or any other criticism, is not the point just now, save in so far as the honest declaration of my thought helps you to understand what I have done. However, it is obvious enough that I have sinned terribly, and in such a way that I may not gain credence for my present utterance ; and it has been quite in vain. Although the door of Pleasure stood open, my heart misgave me, and I could not enter to receive the reward of my treachery. No: although that reward was the certain clasp of your own fair hand, and a close gaze into your pure eyes. Ay, even with you who are to me the princess of angels, on pavements of gold, my sin would find us out to our inevitable doom. To say that "the wages of sin is death," covers all time and space, and makes this earth seem but a pound where God imprisons those whom sin turns to worse than cattle, till the damage is paid. Thus, while I now seem to speed from your arms, can you not see that it is for our infinite good? What would I gain if I purchased your hand with false speech and lived the lie I uttered? Would not my love become your curse, and yours mine? O man of little faith that I was! I gazed Heavenward, although I only beheld the callous clouds and the implacable blue of the sky, while my heart was void of purity, and given up to vanity. And I talked of my Lord, and craved his blessing upon me, even while I closed my conscience with conceit, and shut my soul with a lie. But you, dearest, if you did not see, felt through the mask of my deceit; for the tone of my letters made you sad. Blessed sadness! How I love you for it! But hear me speak more calmly about my thought.

What is the worship of God as he is manifest in the Christ of Nazareth? Is it the acceptance of any scholastic statement or conventional notion as to his being, his place in the Trinity, the authenticity of his miracles, with due appreciation of his self-sacrifice, in particular,— no matter how little one possesses himself,— with tender consideration for the dogmas woven around his name? Or is it simply the genuine love and reverence which such a character as Jesus' naturally inspires in the bosom of all who come within its influence? What more can I say than that I will strive to worship the same Holiness of Spirit which has blessed all nations and tribes with forms of religion in consonance with the merits of each? But look, Jennie, into these things for yourself, and you will see to what extent the world bows down before the true God, and to what extent before the graven images of Madam Demorest, and Spruce, Cut & Co. Excuse the satire, and do not think I blame you; for such as Pluffle, the parrots of the Bible, have not been eager to enlighten you in this matter, in spite of all their talk about the vanities of this wicked world of theirs. I fear you will have to ascend the mountains of Christian Progress yourself. I liked that letter, but there was a careless ring about it that I did not admire. I hope my infidelity to myself did not infect you. You talk of religion as glibly as a school girl about a new book, or as if you, as I, had to look to it for bread. And you speak of sinners being turned into black stones,— excellent comparison, forsooth,— but do you realize what it means? Could you have shared such a fate with me? Ah, you shrink in horror from the thought, and well you may, for you have had a narrow escape. To secure you, such was my impatience that I enlisted in Satan's army and became a theological sharpshooter with a preternatural rifle, and the Bible for a cartridge-box. And I intrenched myself behind a " Rock of ages " of error, and fired at the hearts of the Infidels, so-called. Fortunately, however, most of my cartridges were blank; and, on hearing the empty report, I even laughed myself to scorn. Just think of the killed! Shot through the head with miracles. For a truth, "blessed are the dead which die in the Lord." But I received a severe blow from one Shaft, as you may perceive.

How applicable your parable of Mt. Christian Progress! Can't you make it a little bigger, Jennie? Say Progress alone, or Mt. Restoration. Heaven may be something to regain as well as something new to acquire. 'Tis true that we are infinitely obliged to those who help us to ascend, or guide us thither. But have we not principally to look to our own limbs? Is it not better to be gods ourselves than to remain mere individuals, content with some faint images vouchsafed by Supernal Powers? Thus, in the light of this thought, your mountain looms infinitely high; and behold, that loftiness is in our own minds, and we cannot see where Christ, with his deathless body, ceased to ascend that he might rest content with the sweets of the Universe in halls of glory, surrounded by the countless host of his worshipers, unless it be here in this world. But a fatal spell keeps people from reaching the mystic heights which he ascended with other holy men of old that he might find new treasures for his brethren. And I cannot help comparing the Church, in her superstition, with Charlemagne of the legend. That emperor had rather a plain mistress whose influence over him was due to the possession of a magic ring; and this infatuation continued, even after her death, so that he would not suffer the corpse to be removed from his room. This induced a servant to suspect the presence of witchcraft, and on searching for the charm the ring was found under the tongue. It was removed; and then Charlemagne inquired, for the first time, why the dead body was not taken away at once. See to it, dearest: who knows what fatal witchery is in the tongues of Pluffle, Bungle, and Buzz.

Yours forever,

MALCOLM.

## XII.

### A BRAND NEW PUBLIC INSTRUCTOR.

MALCOLM had barely finished this letter, when some one entered. It was James Singleface, who had come to see some new books which temporarily lay in Malcolm's private room — a present from one of the supporters of the institution. James was looking particularly happy, as if something had occurred to please him, and he was in a talkative mood.

"What do you think of the college, Malcolm?" he began, throwing himself into a chair by the stove and putting his feet upon the mantel.

"Think!" ejaculated Malcolm, turning round. "I think that I am in the wrong box. I am not clay, or, if I were, I should have no desire to be moulded after the pattern of Bungle or Lullaby, and stamped with the seal of the Continental Miracle Protection Association. I leave next week."

"What!" exclaimed James, opening his incredulous eyes, for he was not ignorant of his friend's circumstances. "You are joking. Leave the college, with your rhetorical power! why, my dear fellow, you might make your fortune in the ministry."

"And lose one," resumed Malcolm. "No: the current traditions are sheer frauds in a great measure, and I feel compelled to say so. If you saw a forger cheat a poor man, would you hesitate to interfere?"

"The voice of mock martyrdom again! Rather than go to Heaven on the Church passport, you would give up the whole world! More fool you. If the miracles of the Lord are forgeries, blessed forgeries, say I."

"Blessed poison, virtuous vice, delicious damnation!" exclaimed Malcolm, fairly aroused.

"Why not?" said James, patronizingly. "Where is your Hegel? Does he not teach that all Truth lies in the synthesis of contradictions? Homœopathy proves the blessings of poison. Vicious men have a self-sacrificing virtue, inasmuch as they exhibit in themselves the havoc of vice; and is it not a 'delicious damnation' to be doomed to the pleasures of this wicked world of ours, — eh?"

"You reason well, James; but think again. The success of homœopathy consists in taking the smallest possible quantities of poison; and the self-destruction of the fool attests the extent of his benevolence and the price paid for the lesson taught; and as for your 'delicious damnation,' can you rejoice in the emasculation of soul which it costs?"

"So you believe in a veritable Devil?"

"No: I disown him heartily; but the trouble is he won't disown me, save in so far as he is manifest in the like of you."

"What's the use of talking with you, Malcolm? This trickiness of speech, this absurd sophistry of yours, does not become a Christian and a gentleman. Elevate your spiritual standard. I believe

Christ, and all that savors of 'him crucified.' And our teachers are the select men of the nation. How can they be wrong, and such an undisciplined piece of radical insignificance as you be right?"

"That's the point. I'd rather give myself to the crows than fawn upon the King of kings."

"Ah, Infidelity is so wearing, and there is comfort and dignity in the cloth."

"There's dignity in infinite cruelty, and comfort in the blackfly that buzzes around and, settling, preys on the back of a heifer. Can't you hear poor Io low? Whence the immoralities which disgrace your cloth? Not all the brains of the country, compressed into flattery and unction, can make a whited sepulchre big enough to hide a murdered fact. Stuff, push, cut off, mangle and twist as they will, still the ghastly finger or toe protrudes, and the breath of Gehenna is there. But faugh! I lose my patience, James. Why not be a man like Iago? Confess yourself thus: I've got conscience, it is true, but what the mischief is that? I'll pull it up by the roots, and toss it aside like a weed, if it bothers me at all. Conscience and reason,—ha, ha? Soap-suds and a pipe to blow bubbles with,—rainbows all! Who am I that I should call myself good? Goodness forsooth! 'Tis a blister on the heart and a beggar with a perpetual pleurisy. Out upon thee, Conscience, and thy religious thimble-rigging. If I'd trust thee, thou wouldst turn my days to nails, and drive them all into my flesh. No, no! I'll go in for the fat purse and the sniggering crowd, and it will be strange if I cannot make as good a show as the best."

"Malcolm, you are crazed! What do you mean?"

"Only to make you a better villain."

"What blasphemy!"

"Well, if the cap don't fit, don't wear it. I never take back a gift."

"You appall me with your generosity. But probably, if your thoughts were not the shadows of your own villainy, you would be less extravagant. Why, you actually pray for the restoration of the dead Satan."

"Certainly," replied Lawson. But do justice to my Egotism. If I aspire to be godly, I must, like the Deity, have a Devil to match. The sun must have darkness to shine on, else sunlight were not."

"Well, you beat me. It never occurred to me that God must find a match in his own Lucifer to set off his Divinity to advantage. What a pity that you are not a defender of the Faith!"

"Indeed, I am, but you are not. But excuse me now."

"One moment more, Malcolm. There is something in you, after all, and I would like to get at it. You never have the blues like me. How is that?"

"That's my secret."

"Your secret! Pray reveal it."

"What! a Christian ask a heathen for a revelation? Preposterous!"

"But it is no joke, Malcolm. You rouse a strange interest in me, and, heathen or Christian, I must have your secret."

"Supposing you know it already,—that it is, in fact, an old story,—what then?"

"Never mind. Out with it, and cease to quibble."

"So be it: do you see that skull on the mantel?"

"This?" and James examined it curiously.

"Yes. That piece of mortality was filled with diamonds once, saved from a wreck. I carried them six hundred miles on foot. My comrades lay down and died one after another, and finally I and two others had all the spoil. Our garments turned to rags, and there was no casket so handy as the skull. A weird sight, I tell you, friend, to see those dead sockets dazzling with gems in the tropic sun!"

"How came you to lose your share?"

"It was stolen, whilst I slept, and gambled away."

"But what has this to do with your secret?"

"Much; for, being a fact, it is a parable of God, and therefore a revelation. See those marble halls, those golden spires, those bridges there, and beyond that purple stream, the city on the hill, blushing at the kiss of sunset,— are these not gems given us by our faithful dead and dying? We have each a death's head such as that was, full of value and beauty; but, careless of our boundless wealth, we sleep in a dangerous place, and, behold! our patrimony is gone."

"Strange talk for an infidel!"

"The foolish virgins had no oil in their lamps when the bridegroom came."

"Stranger still. My skull is numb, but hang the lantern-jaws," said the hypocrite, taking refuge in wit.

"O James, familiarity breeds contempt, and you have been an age too long in a divinity school. Why not use your own talents? A clean breast is my secret, and that of all who live in reality, and not in the shadow of another's name, or in the echo of another's thought, or in the phantom glory of by-gone faith. Do you worship Christ truly? If so, you are not only a Christian but a Christ, and if he is God, so are you. And this is the secret of the world as it is revealed to me. Squander not your treasure, but keep an honest lookout. Eternal vigilance is the price of safe travel through this earthly waste."

"What, another sermon! Sold again, and the money paid. What an infidel! We've both got skull on the brain. That's a dead certainty, but you call it a living. And as for diamonds, why, the gems of my intellect shine best in the light of the church. But that may be due to the blackness of the cloth."

"Ghastly mourning, James."

"Glad to hear it. Diamonds look best on dark dresses. But what's the good of them unless you can dispose of them, or get them admired *as yours?* Mine go to the highest bidder. I've two calls, — one to Old Notion and another to Modern Stake: and I think I'll go to the former; for the latter, if not red, is too rare to suit me. But I've rich relations at both. By the way, some new books, I see," and he stopped to look at them. "'Life of the Christ,' Brooklyn, — can't get along without that." And he rattled on, mimicking a showman who stirs up his lions with a long pole; "and, bless me! fifteen versions of the miracles, and Dr. Cumming's exegesis of the Four Beasts and the tenth horn of the Great Dragon, with an essay on pastoral duty annexed! And, ladies and gentlemen, behold Puseyism and Palmistry, and the prophecies of a red-hot radical, cheek by jowl, while Archbishop Manning bursts with papal infallibility, and Conway patronizes Confucius. Good Lord deliver us! man and monkey reconciled by Jonathan Snoozletalk, or all religion placed on a scientific basis, while Channing smiles over the 'Report of the Evangelical Alliance.' And just perceive, Freeman's 'Ladder to Theism' peeps in at the window, and makes love to Jackson's 'Wonders of the Summerland,' while Ficklewits' 'Sympathy of all Creeds' turns up its literary nose at Tom Paine's 'Age of Reason.' And there is 'High Survey,' as amiable as Gulliver at Lilliput, shining in sweet concord with Mr. Vegetable Light, while his old friend Teufelsdhröck points to the stars, and, standing on his coffin, shakes his fist at Death-kingdoms innumerable. On the right is a store of 'Radical Conundrums,' and on the left is Shakespeare, like the Colossus of Rhodes, a fleet of humble vessels sailing beneath. And what have we here? 'Prometheus,' by Jove, a moralist finding his vulture in ladies' eyes, and tortured to death by force of satin and silk; and observe that witty transcendentalist in the middle, baiting a steel-trap for 'American Religion,' while Bradlaugh and Dilke worry the 'Church and State,' like cats playing with a dead rat which they can't eat. And, to crown all, Spurgeon on cigars, Murray on the horse, the impeachment of Andrew Johnson, and the trial of the greatest preacher of the age by his own peers for petty larceny."

And James selected the "Life of the Christ," and

went to his rich relations to preach a creed whose beauty he did not see, and whose letter he despised. The sophist is a Frankenstein : let him have a care concerning his own creation.

"Proud Satan, dead, and gone to swift decay,
No longer stands in man's triumphant way ;
But Carnal Meanness sneaks in paltry snakes
To make unguarded preachers worse than rakes.
Oh, that the Fiend who kept the world in awe,
Should yield to Cant and his base nature's law !

" 'The woman tempted me,' Old Adam said.
But what saith he, who Christian soldiers led,
In name of God who leaves his lofty throne
To live, for sinners' sake, a life-long groan ?
When called by Him to answer for his sin,
That he perforce of Cross may pardon win.
'The woman tempted me,' the saint replies,
And Hell, disgusted, takes to flight and dies.

" 'Our time is come !' the gasping fiends exclaim ;
'What fools were we to risk infernal fame,
When saints themselves disgrace the Christian name.
Oh, that the mind of men could see that we
But Darkness made, that Lovely Light might be !
No hope remains that this disastrous day
Precursor is of aught but filthy prey.
Therefore we imps expire, quite useless grown,
And leave to saints imperial Satan's throne.' "
— *J. Sweep.*

# XIII.

## UNITY IN DIVERSITY.

MALCOLM was left alone, and as he sat wondering how Jennie would receive the avowal of his real sentiments, his eye fell upon some well-used books which had long been his traveling companions. His heart warmed toward them, and he recalled the happy hours he had spent with them while at sea, despite the interruptions of duty. And again he scaled the shrouds, heedless of the angry winds which leaped from their furious chariots and threatened to lift him from his grasp, until at length he reached the royal mast, which smote the sky like a sabre, and sprang upon the creaking yard to gather in the sail, surveying the full form of the ship as she crashed, a host in herself, through the gleaming masses of the sea. But this remembrance soon gave way to another, until finally the books that he had loved took the forms of their authors, and they came near him, as if he, too, belonged to their sacred guild. Yet, scarce had this vision appeared when it faded away, banished, no doubt, by some inferior thought; and as it fled there fled with it the peace of the moment.

"Who am I?" cried he. "What dread mystery is this in which I live and die with the moments that pass? What is this which coils itself around my soul like a snake, and strangles the best of my thoughts as soon as they are born? Alas! I am weak, and there is no completeness for me. I am the Wandering Jew, and those books that I loved are the shades of the dead wives, taunting me with infidelity to their memory. Oh, how I loved you, and worshiped the very words which fell from your lips! Ah, you remember how I picked them up and enshrined them in my heart, where they found a significance not their own! Verily, it is very hard to have sinned, like Ahasuerus. But she remains," he went on, answering for the books, "to recompense you for the loss of the letter; for is she not the best that is left of a thousand generations, the living spirit of the Book of books herself?"

Here that same old serpent who tempted him before warned him not to steal the fire of Heaven. "How absurd," he began, "to waste thy youth amid the vague subtleties of verbal expression! What in the name of all that is pleasant and easy does this metaphysical humdrum amount to? Who art thou that durst aspire, like Lucifer of old, to the dignity of Godhood? Canst thou not see that, far from being even respectable, thou shalt become a great enemy to thy generation? And canst thou not also see, as I have shown thee before, the dismal fate which I foreshadow? Behold thyself on the grim Caucasus of radical isolation, chained to the rock of devotion to a vague idea. For, as sure as God is, and I am that I shall forever be, the Strength and the Force of the Christian Zeus shall take thee in their horrid arms, and rob thy senses of their life. Do not dream, O visionary man, that the loss of the woman thou lovest shall be the sum of thy misery. That were, indeed, but a drop in the river of thy grief. Prepare for a long sojourn in the wilderness of recovery to expiate the sins of thy early youth. Nor is this all. What canst thou, frail one, hope to do in this world, knowing as thou dost that the God of Nazareth, with all his wisdom and will, could find but a few unfortunate women and men to accept the hope and the love he stole from the house of Him whom his very memory deposed?"

"Yet, in his words, blessed are they who are persecuted for righteousness' sake, for theirs is the Kingdom of Heaven."

"No, not half so blessed as they who are poor in spirit; for doomed are they who, in the pride and arrogance of their hearts, aspire to the power and the glory of the existing Zeus. Canst thou not foresee the darkness gather, and forehear the whirr of the birds as they come, borne on the breath of his wrath, to pierce thy bosom with their beaks? Methinks I hear thee cry, in mock-heroic strain, that thou poor *subject* art great as he the *object* King of the world. But, in thy macerated heart, thou shalt feel thyself but a faint echo of the all-pervading voice which sings the song of the universe. No, no. Fly, I pray thee, from thy wild and most fantastic thought; for as the guileless bird, being found among the filchers of the seed, was destroyed, so shalt thou be punished,— yea, even as a scarecrow shalt thou be nailed up on the cross of infamy, even as was he who mixed his groans and his blood with those of the robber and the thief."

"Yet, nevertheless, blessed are they who are persecuted for righteousness' sake, for theirs is the Kingdom of Heaven."

"Ay, indeed. But in this glorious period of honied optimism, social repose, defalcation, and kid gloves, thou shalt not even have the consolation of persecution. For the world has learned that that is as the razor to the beard,—the oftener it is shorn the stronger shall it grow. Thus blank indifference, indiscriminate pity, abject neglect, shall beset thee in thy house, and spill on the ground the cup of thy philanthropy ere it can reach the lips of those who bear the burdens of the world. Ay, doomed and most miserable are they who steal the Father's fire in dark oblivion of the Son's, and give it unto the cold and needy. Slander shall stab them in the dark; Contumely shall crush them in the light; Despair shall blacken the hours that pass; and blind men shall stand upon their eyes. Yet, still shall they live, for their vain and fruitless impulse of love shall grow again as soon as devoured by the eagles of God. And after ten thousand years, ages, days, — for here time and space are not,— shall come the final effort of Fate, when the stars shall be torn from their sockets, and flung like black hail into the fire of the universe, where shall be weeping and wailing and gnashing of teeth."

"But is it not enough,—even if the orbless night vanish in a sea of flame, and with it everything that sense holds dear,—that I will still live? Avaunt, then, Satan, for God, *object* King and almighty though he is, must retain the thought of *his own subject*, and that am I! I am for the moment or the age or the ten thousand ages which I call mine, and I will do as I deem most fit. Thus it is my will to sneer at thee, O Force, and at thee, too, False Sentiment of the times who wouldst string the millstone of base desire round my neck and fling me into the sea of Phantom Convenience. Take, O Zeus, take O World, that which is yours! But I will keep myself to myself, safe and whole, even if you should fling me into the hell of your offended dignity. O ye gods! ye cannot rob me of my will, that is mine forever and ever; and if it is within my power I will dethrone you from your kingdoms of Eternal Indolence and Revenge,— mark you, I will do it. And it will be a joyful sight to see you tumbling, headlong, headlong, from On High; for, behold, the Sun of Righteousness will shine with a new glory and cast a smile upon the whole shower of you, so that Iris alone shall be left to take you in her arms and give you for a shroud the brightest colors of the sky."

# XIV.

## EXCOMMUNICATION.

DRS. Buzz, Bungle, Lullaby, Tightcreed, and other members of the C. M. P. A., concluded that it was not sufficient to fight the good fight in the great Hippodrome, but that that they ought to secure the Latitudinarian Hall, in Upper-class Conversion Street, in order to eradicate any doubt which, notwithstanding the previous victories of the Faith, might linger in the minds of the community concerning the infallible means of redemption at their disposal. So the said hall was hired, and opened to the public by Dr. Bungle, the orator-in-chief of the grand occasion, who, as usual, did himself full justice as a Knight of the Rainbow Creed and moderator of this convention. His text was, "God is love,"—a subject in which he particularly excelled, and certainly the Almighty must have been highly gratified by the glowing tributes paid, not only to himself personally, but to his marvelous works. The auditory, as usual, testified its appreciation of his powers by loud and reiterated applause, and there was no end to the satisfaction of those who had afforded this praiseworthy entertainment.

But since it were needless for us to dwell on so common an occasion as the display of the Rainbow Creed, the peacock of the heavens, we will withdraw our vision from that splendid phenomenon without venturing to describe its wonderful hues. For Progressive and his friends, what with continual intimacy with the Deity, and being admitted to all the secrets of Revelation, have reached a certain pitch of perfection in the description of Divine things which seems quite unattainable by such inferior beings as poor authors, who reside in that blackness farthest from their magnificent Creed. Certainly, we must confess that, in view of the brilliancy of Progressive and his friends, we can well realize how the Children of Israel felt when surprised by Moses, with face on fire with the reflected glory of God, in the act of worshiping a golden calf. So dazzling the vision, with difficulty we keep our countenance. But which of the two, the reader anxiously inquires, is Moses, — Dr. P. Bungle, or the author himself? For the Children of Israel, thus illuminated with a golden calf for a sun, no doubt formed a semi-circle around it not unlike a rainbow, and, according to this, Dr. Bungle, seeing that his Creed subsists wholly by the acceptance of the money of the people, must be Aaron himself, whereas the author, who cannot get anything for his work, or anybody to believe it, is more apt to resemble the great prophet in the act of holding up the "Ten Commandments." But, in any case, the Rainbow Creed is a hard thing to describe without special assistance from On High, so we must even run the risk of being taken for idolators capering around a graven image, and let it go at that.

Malcolm, who had attended every meeting, and

carefully listened to all that was said, deplored in an elaborate epistle addressed to the Faculty his inability to make their views of religion harmonize with his. We merely give from memory, as we had not the good fortune to receive the production, the gist of the same. He declared, firstly, that he was principally occupied by the stupendous miracle of his own being, and that in such wise that he had no reason for or need of any other to support or help his belief in God; and he wondered why his teachers gave themselves so much concern about the miracles of the Jews. Secondly, he so respected the inscrutable mystery of Life, not to mention religion at all, that he did not think it a fit subject for mechanical utterance and immature, hap-hazard oratory. Thirdly, his study and research, limited as they were, were yet sufficient to inform him that all religions, in so far as they merited the name "religion," were one in spirit and purpose, but only inadequately appreciated and preached by their individual supporters; and that, considering his recognition of this simple Truth, he did not think it worth his while to favor any one sect, for he could not do it save to the prejudice of another. "Moreover," he added, "I cannot believe in any sect, section, or slice of the whole Truth, and pertain to it exclusively after the manner of denominationalists, without thereby doing simple religion an injury. I think it a sin to be partial: to be impartial is to be just and holy." And shortly after this, in a fourth statement, he declared that he saw no reason why Jesus should be called God, save in so far as he, being a good man who did the best he could for his kind, was entitled to their recognition and respect. "In which case," he went on, "I cannot in common logic separate the genuine man from the genuine God. Both are one in the same holy Spirit of Reform in which Jesus intimated that he lived and loved, praying that all others might share the same unity." Fifthly, he told his teachers that his conviction of immortality came to him through his own experience, and not through the tradition of the phenomenal death, resurrection, and dematerialization of Jesus.

The assembled representatives of the Christian God, it is needless to say, were not particularly gratified by this unexpected ebullition of their young Lucifer.

"'Stupendous miracle' of his being!" exclaimed Tightcreed. "Who the Devil is he? Excuse me, gentlemen, but positively the blasphemy of the rascal is beyond all precedent."

"I do not blame you at all," said Bungle, smiling; for he enjoyed, as he said, a slant at the theologians. "It is far beyond the president's. But there is some truth in what he says, after all."

"Just enough," said Lullaby, "to make it pass with the few turbulent spirits which hang on the outskirts of the Lord's army, as eager to help the enemy as the friend, according to the whim of the moment. It is not in the nature of things that the vague ideology which this young man represents can ever be popular or effective. I must say I prefer the clumsy yet logical exactitude of the declared enemy of the Church. However, this vehement youth will soon change his fancies for the stable articles of the Faith. Our most successful clergymen had to struggle through various phases of Infidelity in order to gain their present renown."

"You do not refer to the thirty-nine, I hope," said Bungle, enjoying the situation.

"No," replied Lullaby, "we cannot expect the talented youth of our time to run in the old grooves of Christian ordinance. Yet it is not too much to expect that they will show some moderation for their own sake, and a little respect for their superiors."

"But, Lullaby, you see," said Bungle, "the subjective radical impulse is very strong, and, so far as I can see, if Christ is the Ideal Person whom we are all to recognize, we, in spite of various traditions, must stand to a great extent upon a subjective philosophy. Now, then, if Christianity is the real spirit of love, and not a mere name covering a special theology, upon what else can we base our action?"

"I do not like," said Tightcreed, with a look of fire, "that way of looking at things. If the isolated fact of the individual Jesus' atoning sacrifice falls, where are we? I must say it is not in accordance with my sympathy with the fallen state of humanity, nor in keeping with my career as a minister of the Gospel, to tolerate any innovation of the kind suggested. So I beg of you, gentlemen, if ye be worthy servants of the Lord, to close this matter at once by expelling this unfortunate man from the institution. As soon as I saw him, I felt that he was in no way fitted to do service in the Vineyard. This is the dictate of my own good sense, which is altogether unbiased by any of your new-fangled objective and subjective speculations, which whimsical attempts to penetrate the mysteries have nothing at all to do with our profession as I understand it."

"But, friend Tightcreed," said Bungle, "consider the tendency of the age. I see little harm in the lad. He is only carried away by a sudden perception of a great truth, which for the sake of opportunity he will have to tone down somewhat. Very few young men, I observe, remain long on the visionary stage upon which a generous, though mistaken impulse brings them to act. The common sense of the world is too strong to admit of long continuance amid the mists of juvenile enthusiasm. I think, as I said before, that you had better give way a little, Brother Tightcreed, and let him stay."

"I dare not," said Tightcreed, in a rage; "his conduct is too exasperating, too provocative of rebellion among his classmates. I am sorry, very sorry, but go he must."

Dr. Bungle sighed, for he had a good heart; yet he could not do as he pleased in his present uncomfortable position. He feared that Christ, the sun of his righteousness, might go out and leave him, poor raindrop, without a vestige of color.

"Gentlemen," said he, "I protest, in Christ's name I protest, against the tyranny which would deprive the institution of a noble-minded youth whose satire is only the result of a deep feeling of the inadequacy of any single intellectual statement to contain the stupendous mystery of God. Leave him yet awhile to himself, and no doubt the ripen ing of his intellect, and the prudence which cometh with years, will make him one of our most esteemed brethren in the Faith."

"I have spoken once and forever in regard to this matter," said the terrible Tightcreed.

"But hear me, Brother Tightcreed," said Lullaby, energetically; "while I agree with you in thus reprobating the strange conduct of this youth, considering it as you do, a rank instance of disloyalty to Christ, I think, with Brother Bungle, it might be more prudent to pass over this essay as a burst of boyish petulance. It really is not worth our while, as I have frequently urged, to fret ourselves about the puerilities of the period. Christianity, beyond all doubt, has too strong a hold on the affections of the people to be affected in the least by the frantic attempts of Infidelity to cast it off. But, brethren, do as you please; far be it from me to interfere with your consciences. By the way, here comes Brother Buzz. Let us have a word from him."

That dignitary being shown the manifesto, declared at once his opinion of the matter.

"Gentlemen," he began, with a profound sigh, "here we have the most melancholy instance of heresy which has ever darkened our Church. The whole character of our religion is most slanderously defamed or perverted in such a way as to make angels weep. Do not hesitate to make an example of this headstrong and most unruly youth, who, notwithstanding our past indulgence and the kindness of Brother Crisp, thus repudiates the faith which giveth eternal life. Let us rise at once in the firm warmth of our righteous indignation and dismiss him from our Church, where I am afraid he has sown the seed of the worst Infidelity."

"But, dear Buzz," said Bungle, "don't you exaggerate a little? Read again his hasty, yet not wholly impertinent remarks. There is far more to him than you think. There is an intuitive logic in them that demands some forethought."

"What is the use of reasoning," replied Buzz, "when a man openly and resolutely denies all faith in the special lordship of Jesus, in the miracles and atonement, as taught from time immemorial? For my part, the less we say, and the sooner we get rid of him, the better for us and the people whom we serve. In some respects, I confess, I rather like the young man. He says a good thing once in a while, but this dreamy skepticism of his, this indecent, slap-dash and random vagueness of character, is altogether incompatible with the discretion and gravity demanded by the denominational interests, which, to tell the truth, are rather low just now; but, no doubt, the most resolute preaching of Christ will bring them up again."

"Yet we must be more of Christs ourselves, if I may say so," said Bungle. "I am tired of prayer-meetings. Is there no other means of redemption?"

"I see nothing before us," replied the persistent Buzz, "but to remain consistent with ourselves, as Christian ministers, and faithful to the denominational interests. God has hardened the heart of modern Infidelity. We can no other than use our power in behalf of His people. Let us, then, stretch forth the rod of 'the Word.' The plague must fall on the obdurate Egyptian."

"But be sure your plague falls on the right person," said Bungle. "There are many kinds of Infidelity nowadays."

"How can we, gentlemen," returned Buzz, "with Christ for our guide, err in this matter? Respect for his name, and regard for the peace of society, compel us to banish this man from our communion."

"I suppose, then," said Bungle, languidly, "you must have your way. But I scarcely like to part with him. He is better than you think."

"I will take the responsibility," cried Tightcreed.

"And I too," said the eager Buzz; "the repose of society must be guaranteed."

"And you may be right after all," concluded Lullaby. "The egotism of Lawson is positively alarming. What a pity that our faithful friend Crisp should have been so deceived in him! Pluffle ought to have used his influence to better advantage. Not, however, that I think Lawson a bad young man; but this unfortunate streak, this unfortunate streak, this atrocious levity and ape-like malevolence, properly termed satire, which vitiates his entire being! Alas! Mr. Carlyle has much to answer for; and those men of Concord, when, oh, when shall a limit be put to their influence? Even the most beautiful spirits are tainted by their fatal example."

"I hope," returned Buzz, "you do not blame my illustrious friend, Mr. High Survey, for the delinquencies of the period. He has outlived his radicalism, and now sees the propriety of becoming a declared advocate of prayer, as becometh the recipient of the highest honors of literature."

"Of course not," cried Lullaby. "But I doubt whether the beautiful picture of dignity and repose he now exhibits will fully atone for the Infidelity of his earlier years. But, not to mention him, we have much to be thankful for. Let us unite in prayer."

After this a letter of excommunication was written and sent to Malcolm.

So much for P. Bungle as raindrop. Let us end with a word about him as rainbow in full. This was essentially a man of his times, a sort of theological Disraeli, who, with the most finished jugglery of tongue, could conciliate all sides of the Church with a breath, and compel them to echo his praises as the greatest light of the age, the most brilliant specimen of humility extant. He was the leader-in-chief and grand master of the great Independent Spirit Navigation Denomination, being the admiral of six squadrons of humble vessels. He was a Calvinist, a Unitarian, a Liberal Christian, a Universalist, a Republican, and a Phrenologist. Nor did he neglect agriculture and the fine arts. There is no word in the dictionary or elsewhere more adequate to express his theological merit than "Rainbow." We can see him now, overarching the world from Dan to Beersheba, an object of admiration to the children of all schools, who, as soon as he appears upon the horizon, rush to see him spread himself. He was all things to all men, and more especially to the women, who, as we have already said, are more sensitive to the operation of the

Spirit than men; and he was just as good and as great a man as you could expect a Christian in his position to be,—a splendid character spoiled by one or two lasting lies, a koh-i-noor diamond with a flaw.

We actually believe—such was the astounding liberality of this knight—that if it had been he, instead of Luther, who inaugurated the Reformation, there never would have been any marked difference between Protestants and Roman Catholics. He would have argued with the Pope in this wise: "Now, my dear father Leo, you must know that I have your interest at heart. You cannot but see the radical tendencies of the times and the necessity of being a little less strict in your views. Give way a little. Men are necessarily different from one another. One likes fish and another likes flesh. Just look at their heads: here is a bullet, there is a pumpkin. You must adapt yourself to circumstances and give up this absolution business. It will be the death of you."

What do you think Leo would have said to this harangue?

We think we hear him say, "Come to my arms, my dear Progressive, you are a man after my own heart. Just take this cardinal's hat, and forget the Absolution for a day or two. We will attend to it as soon as we can get time. Don't fuss about it. Whatever is, is right. As you yourself say, some need flesh and others need fish. You cannot treat an ass like a sheep. I happen to be awfully hard up just now, and must keep up appearances. What would all the grannies say, if I took away this blessed means of redemption?" Here old Leo would wink jesuitically, and the Rev. P. Bungle would walk off with the cardinal's hat, and not know whether to wink or not.

Mr. Mob is the Pope of the present day, and well rewards all that will pander to his variable theological and psychological fancies. These cards are so handy, and the magic table is so exquisitely constructed. Words do so easily turn themselves into bread, and illustrations are splendid bridges for difficult places! But Mr. Mob grumbles and asks, "What am I to do if there be no one to tell me about the immortality of my individual consciousness? I cannot get along without a hint or two on that subject." And we reply, "Mr. Mob, do you know what became of the boarder that did not pay his board-bill?" Mr. Mob grins; for he thinks we are making fun of him. But when we tell him that Eternal Law, not to say the Eternal Person, has a knack of numbering such defaulters among the goats who do not obtain a seat at the divine table, he looks augry, and throws an ominous glance on the mud in which he stands, while we, remembering Prometheus and the Cross, know enough to hold our tongue.

We humbly resign to Drs. Lullaby, Buzz, Bungle, and Pluffle the privilege of telling him about the angel throng on high : we have enough to do to draw attention to the angel throng of Virtues here below. Those ten commandments must be resuscitated. Who will join the league that Mr. Shaft proposed to that laudable end?

How absurd to base the Eternal Verities on the wonderful doings of those who lived thousands of years ago! The dream about the image that Daniel told to Nebuchadnezzar is applicable to the empire of Christianity. Verily there is much clay intermixed with the iron of its feet, and fall it surely shall, unless steps are immediately taken to remove the crumbling earth, and supply a stronger material. Half-way measures are bungling. The clay must be taken away, and carefully, too, lest the image topple suddenly over on our heads.

But there is some weird influence at work, akin to the magic of the ring of Charlemagne's mistress, that keeps us from seeing the havoc of decay. For with greater zeal than ever we find people devoting themselves to priest, confessional, surplice and candlestick, as if the sun of Knowledge had ceased to shine upon them. What does it all mean? There must be some fearfully anaconda or scorpion-like unfaithfulness to the Good in the nursery of the Lord, so that those who enter there become fascinated, and then, being well anointed by the oil of its tongue, are devoured whole, or stung to death. Priests are often lionized; may they not also become like the Serpent they rail against? But such things dwell not in places of light and repose, being the natives of the black pitch-pools which Doré paints so powerfully. And where does that darkness end? As there is no beginning, so is there no end to it. There are spots upon the sun, and, as the poet says, "there is a crack in everything God makes." This is the crack the darkness streams through and brings with it the horrible things Dante saw in the flight of imagination which carried him into the realms below. The coincidences between the conceptions in John's revelations, in Swedenborg's, and in Dante's are worthy of note. How natural that the lustful and the vile should assume the forms of death's heads, hairy spiders, and slimy griffins to the eyes of the pure; and yet we can lay down our pens and go and sin again, and laugh as if nothing had happened.

The Rainbow Knights make a terrible leap on the steeds of their eloquence when they spring across the chasm that separates the old school from the new. Happy tact! what ease of transition from degrading superstition to half-incubated philosophy! But the chasm, owing to the logic of events, is growing daily wider and wider and more difficult to be leaped. The knights carefully avoid emphasizing the "mystic efficacy of the blood," which is the peculiar characteristic of Christianity as opposed to rational deism. For that would be to stumble in the leap and spoil the effect of the show; or, not to lose Scriptural phrase, that were to sew the patch on the old garment wrong side out, and exhibit too plainly the wear and tear of the old bottles into which they pour the new wine of modern thought. "But," as James Singleface forcibly remarked to Malcolm, "what is the use of telling people what they do not want to hear. When I preach to radical societies, I alter the word 'Christ' into 'Goodness,' and when I preach to conservative, I slip in 'Christ' again, and all parties are pleased."

"James," asked Malcolm in reply, "did you ever read the story of the old man, the boy, and the ass?"

"Yes: what about it?"

"Don't you see the application?"

"No."

"Your object in being a minister, as I understand it, is to bring souls to Christ, or to God, which is the same thing to you. In that case do not try to please everybody. What would Jesus have been had he been a Sadducee to the Sadducees, a Pharisee to the Pharisees, and so on? You are delegated primarily to bring your own soul to eternal life, or *vice versa*. See that it does not slip through your fingers on the road. There is only One to be pleased."

"What an egotist you are, Malcolm!"

"So was Jesus, James."

"But he was God."

"If he was, what are you and I?"

"Ha, ha, ha! you're ready for an insane asylum."

"What is God, James?"

"Love."

"Are you hate?"

"I can't say that I am, Malcolm."

"Did you never hear that love was life?"

"Yes: a rhetorical delusion."

"Not at all! He who loveth eternal things is eternal love, and he who loveth them not is without eternal life, or, what is the same thing, without God in the world. People are just that which the character of their love makes them. The best philosophy, the best conduct of life, is to seek to know the best thing and to love it with all one's might. Therein lies the thriftiness of the soul which builds her house upon a rock."

"But all that is very impracticable. We must attend to things around us," said James.

"Certainly, that love is not dead: its life is virtue, unceasing pursuit of the eternal, and common sense is its best friend and helper. I look upon things from an eternal point of view,— you from a temporal. All things are divine, and nothing is more divine than being truly sensible men and women. A seer is not a visionary."

"That sounds very well, but there is nothing substantial to it. I want a tangible God."

"And you have one in your pocket."

"But, be serious a moment, Malcolm, what would we do without the house of refuge given us by our Lord and Master?"

"What would the soft-backed hermit crab do without the old, worm-eaten conch into which it crawls and hides itself, all but the claws, which protrude ready to catch unsuspecting marines?"

"That's a good joke, Malcolm. I'll laugh at it to-morrow after breakfast. The bell has rung for prayers. It is my turn to officiate." And the young priest withdrew, and Malcolm had a good laugh all to himself.

Poor Bungle! thou hast shown thy white feather, and clucking as thou hast raised thy swan-like wings, thou hast gathered thy chickens under them. O Hub! thou art a hubbub, and in the Tower of

Babel behold thy fate! Thou thinkest to build a tower of words that will touch the skies. But God confuses thy tongues so that thy work remains always barely begun. Thou lookest up: why not look within?

Hypocrisy seems to have become quite fashionable, not to say respectable, but more worthy of its name than ever. The fact is, some people are born with so great a genius for acting that they naturally find — seeing that respectability precludes a theatrical career — a stage in the Church adapted to their merits; or, if their views are particularly broad and liberal, they grow quite optimistic, and act upon the assumption that "all the world is" not only "a stage" of renown, but also "an oyster," mystically provided for their enjoyment. And as some animals — the hermit crab, for instance — take to cast-off shells, they adopt what is left of the expression of the grand character they love to represent. Nor is this acting of theirs altogether the result of inherent weakness, as in the case of the crab. On the contrary, it appears to rise from the strongest regard for others, especially for ladies, — a regard so devout and tender-hearted as almost to deserve the name of Liberal. We might account for it on the hypothesis that they have already attained salvation, even in this world, as the elect of the Lord, yet naturally growing tired of the great, but perhaps monotonous, sweetness of their Heavenly Life, seek to vary it with sundry carnal pleasures, even as Bagdad's Caliph, tired of his luxurious halls, went out in disguise to seek adventures in poor localities.

## XV.

### JENNIE'S ANSWER.

MALCOLM was put out of suspense by the following letter:—

DEAREST MALCOLM, BRAGVILLE, FRIDAY.

How am I to answer you? Your letter is bewildering. Give up Christ, give up the Church? No: you cannot be so deluded. Father will be greatly disappointed, — and what am I to do? To whose voice shall I give ear? I am on the road to betterment, and dread the consequences of looking back. But I shall keep my eyes open, as you advise, and resist the impulse of the moment. There is truth in your parables, and I will possess myself of it. How could you so deceive us, lulling us into a feeling of security, and then betray us in this way! Yet, how can I blame you, seeing that love for me was at fault in one instance, and love for the Truth in the latter?

My affection for you is still unaltered. Have no fear. I shall never forsake you for a difference in creed. Your mind, fired by a love of Truth, has only lighted a torch whereby I can better see to read your character. But that is still a mystery to me; for, although your words are luminous, I feel as if I were looking through a window into the dark. I own what you say about the church is not wholly untrue. She must have some weakness, else there would be no necessity for her continual self-recommendation. Is Christianity a criminal, liable to conviction, in whose favor evidence must be collected and adduced? But, on the other hand, remember the good which the gospel has done, and think what the world would have been without it. No doubt the church, in so far as she has relied on human instruments alone, has failed to realize her great ideal, Christ, in this earthly existence, which realization has been her mission from the first. And it is possible that people have been too thirsty, too eager for refreshment, to heed the impurities which inevitably gather in all the earthly vessels appointed to contain the waters of salvation. Therefore it may be well for you, or any other truthful person, to point them out that they may be removed by the guardians of the Faith. But why not fully accept the idea of invisible fraternity which you admire in the church, and, acting upon it, avoid all dispute, in that you harmonize with its best representation? You have little indulgence for the infirmities of your kind. What though the minor tenets of the church fall from time to time, like the effete feathers of a bird whose flight once depended on them? The bird is all the better for their loss, and sings more sweetly as she flies to and from the heavens above. And you deride superstition! But shall there not be a vague beyond to every ascending soul? You say Mount Progress is infinitely high. Yet who gets beyond the region of simple goodness? Heaven is there, and where else can Christ be? O Malcolm, I fear people talk too much about Progress! That word, as well as the name of Christ, has become the property of cant. You have not heard all the rose-water talk about it, especially in regard to liberty and women, current in Bragville here.

You make me ashamed of my vanity in asking you to procure so expensive a shawl. I send it back, at a reduction. Keep the money yourself, as you may need it. It may be long before father will consent to our union. I am sorry to say that he is still under the influence of Dr. Pluffle, whose true character I know and despise.

It may be, dear Malcolm, that you have studied too hard, and thereby affected the balance of your mind. You have heard how Dr. Ethereal Smart injured himself. You cannot be too careful of yourself. I often wish you could realize the efficacy of prayer. But I will pray for you, no matter how much you say against it, — in word as well as in persistent effort, and the answer shall not be wanting.

The longer I dwell on the singularity of your views, the

easier I think it is for you to adopt a more moderate way of expressing yourself. Can you not even be a liberal Christian, like the brilliant Mr. Piouswit? Yet, under all circumstances, adhere to the Truth, as you best understand it; and whatever you do will not be far in the wrong. I know well how anxiously you will strive to reach the perfection you see before you. Therefore I do not despair of a happy termination to the present perplexity. I have not only read the books you sent, but striven to keep up with you in the study of theology. Yet I did not tell you this before, as I wished to surprise you. I hope and pray you will carefully consider the step you have taken. Believe me to be yours forever.

JENNIE.

Malcolm, though not unmoved by the contents of this letter, could not but admire the tone of it. He had forced her to think radically, and he was astonished at the extent of her knowledge. "Poor child!" said he to himself, "thy soul is superior to its surroundings, and would fain, if it only had light sufficient, free itself entirely from them. The lily has been shaken, and some of the aphides have fled. How can I continue to help her? Words are of but little use in this matter. I wish I were beside her again. But that is impossible. I cannot go to her till I hear from her father. It is sheer nonsense to coax ourselves into the belief that there is any stability in air castles. And she would give me all she had to bestow, — no: I cannot accept of her bounty. I have painfully discovered that Earnest Endeavor is not yet dead. Him shall I invoke to my aid, and, backed by him, there is no such thing as failure. Therefore, here be it resolved: I shall work, and leave all else to the Good. Words are only the dust which is raised by the chariot wheels of Deeds, and it blinds the loungers on the way. I will leave the pen to those that need it. There is enough vain, incoherent speech in the world without the addition of mine. And if my hand findeth nothing else to do there still remains to me the spade of manly labor. That shall be my stay. But what is this phantom discontent that I feel within me, and from which I cannot escape? Discontent, — what is it but the absence of all *con*-tent? Sheer emptiness. Am I empty or am I full? Alas! I have been more than half empty, but I will be it no longer, wife or no wife. I will open the doors of my being, and the heavens and the earth, — all shall stream in, and I will be the universe myself, and the spade shall be my Atlas."

# XVI.

## AN OLD STORY RETOLD.

FINALLY Malcolm sat down and wrote to Jennie, telling her to look within and be sure to think well for herself before accepting the thought of another, and that, if she would but earnestly seek, she would be as likely to receive inspiration from God as any of the ancient prophets. For the rest, he told her his happiness would be to assist her in every conceivable way that was compatible with the present circumstances, as he would not like to visit her until he had heard from her father. Then he wrote to her father.

He had no sooner finished the above task than Ernest Hart, one of the best young men in the establishment, knocked at the door, and, Malcolm opening it, he came in. He came with the intention of inviting him to a conference meeting, where he had been asked to deliver a short discourse.

Malcolm went, and had another opportunity of seeing the consequence of telling folk what they do not want to hear. This Mr. Hart was guilty of the folly of dwelling dangerously long upon Bunsen's ideas, which, if adopted by the Church, might help her much. A certain chapter in "God in History" had taken Mr. Hart's fancy, and he was about to propound what he gathered from it to a prayerful auditory which met for mutual consolation and instruction.

Mr. Hart spoke as follows: "Abraham is a genuine historic character, and was the reformer of his day. The story of his attempted sacrifice of his son plainly points to that fact. Hear the true version of the story: Abraham belonged to the Semitic race, the Hebrews forming one portion of it, and the Carthaginians another. The Semites were remarkable for the vigor of their superstition. This characteristic showed itself in the offering up of their offspring upon the altars of the gods. The Carthaginians, even in the most flourishing period of their national existence, were addicted to that horrible mode of worship; and that the Hebrews were likewise given to the same is evident from the words, 'And he defiled Topheth, which is in the valley of the children of Hinnom, that no man might make his son or his daughter to pass through the fire to Molech.'" (2 Kings xxiii. 10.)

"However barbarous the above rite may seem to us to-day, it was not without good in its time. It was a natural consequence of the intensity of the Semitic religious consciousness, even as witch and heretic burning was a proof of the zeal of our forefathers. The Semite gave the best thing he had to his god, and if his faith had not been strong enough to enable him to do so we might still be in the power of a superstition worse even than that of the Druids from whom we are descended. The Semitic faith being the strongest, according to the necessary struggle for existence which prevails among all animate things, necessarily swallowed up the weaker, and fed itself upon the life that was in them. Creeds are thrown pell-mell into the world and grow fat or lean, according as they succeed in strangling and devouring one another. I never see a pond which contains many kinds of fish without seeing in their contests for supremacy, the fights and bickerings of not only all the Christian sects, but of all the religions of the world. Churches are not only houses of God, but fortresses of God, and are continually exchanging shots.

"The Semitic faith itself is like the mountain torrent, which, on leaving its rocky bed, loses its savage character, and, taking in lesser streams as it advances, slowly and surely widens into a fair and navigable river. During the first Christian century there was a conflux of faiths in which the Semitic element predominated, as our religion is essentially Jewish, and neither Greek nor Roman, although all time has made it what it now is.

"The voice of God in religious custom and prejudice naturally calls on Abraham, as he has been brought up to worship Molech, to offer up Isaac, his most beloved child, on the altar of this deity. Not only this voice, but all outward circumstances combine to urge this duty upon him. If he fails to do it which is only what his pious neighbors are daily doing, he shall be scorned and upbraided as a skeptic who loves his son better than his God.

"The struggle is great in the heart of the parent. He naturally asks himself if Molech really can be so exacting as to rob him of the object that he holds dearest on earth. Molech prevails. The child is taken from play, and goes with his father to Mount Moriah. The wood at last is gathered and piled into a heap: all is now ready for the consummation of the terrible deed. What a picture? The tender boy lies upon the fagots, his plaintive cry, mingling with the rustle of the leaves of the trees, sinks deep into the parental heart, his dark Hebrew eyes, suffused with tears, look up appealingly to the father's face, who, attired in his priestly robes, stands with uplifted knife, ready to plunge it into his quivering bowels. Hark! an angel calls from an opening in the sky. It is the voice of God in Abraham's reason which tells him to sheathe his knife and release his son, as Justice requireth not superfluous blood.

" Accept the lesson. Is God not more likely to call from within, from the place where Jesus said the kingdom of Heaven lay, than from the clouds above our heads? In what other way has any man in any age or in any clime triumphed over the errors of the Past, and given ear to the promptings of a higher enlightenment? Abraham was a radical, even as the late John Brown, who has given to the gallows a meaning akin to that of the Cross. To which voice shall we listen, to that of the Living or to that of the Dead?"

If a bombshell had fallen into the midst of that prayerful assembly and exploded, greater consternation could not have been exhibited. Gradually the questions obtruded themselves into reflecting brains: Was Jehovah a mere myth? Did not an actual angel call to Abraham from the sky? Was Abraham more remarkable for "poor human reason" than the faith which had been the subject of a billion sermons? Could it be that Drs. Lullaby, Bungle, Buzz, and the whole Rainbow Creed World were wrong and this daring youth was right? Deacons opened wide their sleepy eyes and gazed, with eager solicitude depicted on their faces, upon the tender youth present to ascertain if they had been injured by this bolt of heresy. Old ladies looked alarmed and clasped their prayer-books convulsively, as if they thought the Evil One had appeared upon the platform. The young people seemed bewildered, and the children tittered and stared. A long pause followed the sitting down of Mr. Hart.

At last, in a far-away corner of the hall, a shrill voice broke the appalling silence. It was little red-headed Brown's, who, inwardly exultant over this chance of knocking a heresy on the head and thereby adding to his reputation as a defender of the faith, had arisen, and was now shouting, "I believe in the faith of Abraham, of Isaac and of Jacob, as it is given us here in this book of books which has been handed down to us from generation to generation of saints, unaltered and intact. Without the inspired contents of this volume (and he raised his Bible aloft), O brethren in the Lord, where would we be? What hold or stay would we have in this wicked world which surges round us like a sea." And so he went on for half an hour in a most doleful tone.

A number followed him and talked diffusely about breaking "the great compass," "only guide," and so forth. When the meeting was over, if little red-headed Brown had just landed on the wharf after saving at the risk of his own life that of another, the by-standers could not have shaken his hand more cordially than did the "humble followers" on this occasion, while Mr. Hart, whose heresy was only an open respect for a self-evident truth, was scowled upon and regarded with looks of pity. Malcolm was not astonished. He had seen the same thing occur before.

As Ernest had to go in a different direction, Malcolm returned home in company with Rev. Hezekiah Graves.

That gentleman taught the boys to write funeral sermons. He was a well-meaning man, but very superstitious.

He was profoundly shocked by the heresy of Mr. Hart. "Verily," said he to Malcolm, "I am much grieved to find all my labor upon him has been lost. Had it been you or some of the others, it would not have troubled me so much; for you are not gifted to be of comfort to bereaved friends. He can pray beautifully. What unction! what a voice! I fear he will fall into the hands of the radical Unitarians, for we cannot suffer so open a heretic in our ranks. Alas! many are called, few are chosen. To deny Father Abraham, too, — to throw away his faith at the bidding of Bunsen. 'Tis too bad."

Scarcely able to repress the laugh that rose to his lips, Malcolm hardly knew what to say to this commander of the faithful. Finally, looking up at his lofty forehead, he contrived to say reflectively, "I have always thought, Dr. Graves that if you had less veneration you might have held a much higher position in the denomination."

"I hardly think so," replied Dr. Graves with a shudder. "Veneration has been of immense service to me at funerals." And he expressed as much as to say, "That in my opinion is not the least important part of the profession."

# XVII.

## THE MODERN STAKE.

THAT evening Hart rushed into Malcolm's room with the following letter in his hand:

CHURCH OF THE SEVENTY-FIVE APOSTLES.

MR. ERNEST HART,

Rev. Hezekiah Graves and a delegation of three from Hortatorial Hall, Tabernacle Street, have lodged a complaint with us against you.

It appears that you have wantonly, and in the most unheard of manner, despised or misconstrued the letter of sacred writ: in one word, that you have with your infidel views so shocked the religious sensibilities and sacred convictions of a number of our people as to make it incumbent upon us, the guardians of the Faith, to let you know that, in justice to the cause to which we have devoted our lives, we can no longer tolerate your presence in Huberton University.

Hoping, trusting, praying that you will in time be graciously permitted to see the error of your ways, we remain dutifully,

Yours in Christ,

ORATONE BUZZ, D.D.
SIMON LULLABY, LL.D.
JOSIAH TRAMMELE.
ABLE THUNDERHEAD, D.D.
BENJAMIN TIGHTCREED.

A long pause followed the reading of this letter. Malcolm spoke first, saying: " That's why, Ernest, so many ministers seem as if they had been created by measure, and cut into pieces from five to six feet long, each piece being set up to sprout in the sun like willow fence-posts."

"Yes, all originality is pruned off, and the bare stem is left with little or no verdure. P. Bungle is the only one in the Independent Spirit Navigation Denomination who has any claim to genius, and even he is spoiled by his devil-pacificatoriness. But, fortunately, I can't complain. I've got a good situation on 'The Weekly Flapjack,' the first Darwinian paper in the country."

"Indeed!" exclaimed Malcolm. "I told you it was impossible to get persecuted, unless by one's own self, in these advanced times."

"How you do talk, Malcolm! To say the least, the proposed insertion of God in the Constitution is frightfully ominous. We must be on our guard; but, with Darwin for our guide, I see nothing to hinder complete emancipation from Christian superstitions."

"I wish you joy with your emancipations; but don't forget that Christ reconciles man with God, while Darwin reconciles man with monkey. Whose atonement do you prefer?"

"For shame, Malcolm, to ridicule the Sacred Truths of Science!"

"For which, Ernest, you are ready to undergo martyrdom on 'The Weekly Flapjack.' O ye shades of Cranmer, Latimer, and Huss, what say ye to this? There is not enough Religion left to hang an infidel. But excuse me, Ernest, I have to read Shaft's 'Straw King.'"

# XVIII.

## TRANSMIGRATION.

THE professors were benevolent; and alive themselves to all the advantages of Supernaturalism so-called, they sought to make the students share in this Alladin's lamp of spiritual illumination. "But somehow or other," as Dr. Buzz pompously remarked, "some young men have a most incomprehensible antipathy to the miracles, ascribable alone to the eccentricities of the brilliant leaders in modern literature." Yet again and again, with vigor ever renewed, but ever fruitlessly expended, the professors besieged the minds of the skeptical. Such as James Singleface and little Brown, who "could not afford to be anything but sound Christians," and only thought to follow the example of their teachers, gave them no trouble at all. Now, had these two been able to lay bare the contents of their minds, they might have said, "No: it cannot be that Dr. A., whose pen, employed by the first newspapers, nets him a hundred dollars an hour, is wrong; or Dr. B., who has written twenty books, enumerating all the steps from Atheism to Theism; or is it possible that Dr. C., with his congregation of five thousand, and steeple four hundred feet above the level of the sea, can be wrong, preaching, as he does, in a pulpit not unlike the throne of Delhi, while gothic windows, grand, vast, circular, vomit rainbows on the floor? No; a murrain upon your atheism. We shall stand up for Jesus." So Singleface and Brown parted their hair in the middle, and became men after the Faculty's own heart.

Now, there were in the college six students, at least, who would not accept Jehovah's crowns of glory, all ablaze as they were with miracles for gems, and fit for immediate wear. Nay, they even refused to try them on, to the mingled annoyance and compassion of the monarchs of the Church. Loaves and fishes, Lazarus, Gabriel, and Jonah, and many other inviting objects, were duly tendered on the golden salvers of custom and tradition. But no! The infidels said they were Republicans, and protested against all royalty, including even that of the great I Am. Malcolm and his friend, Arthur Bestface, the type of Christian sincerity, told them repeatedly that it was not worth their while to contend about this small matter; but they were determined to have their own way, and so capsized the said salvers whenever they were offered them, and trampled the gems beneath their feet. Ernest Hart was the ringleader; but he ought to have known better. O Ernest, the student, if he wishes to do good, has something else to do besides smashing images. Baby Tom put out the eyes of his sister's doll, and got well whipped for his ill-nature.

Finally the professors concluded that it was high time to give the Apollyon of heresy a deadly thrust; and they stretched forth their hands for the sword of Logic (for that of Good Faith lay broken on the ground). But the enemy was prepared. Ernest Hart drew caricatures of the anticipated thrust, and pasted them on the chapel door,— to this effect: Supernaturalism represented as a balloon, spun like a top over a few odd trees; and the professors were the aeronauts, doing their best to land, despite the opposition of the whirlwind. The grappling-irons were the miracles, and the trees were the students. Dr. Lullaby had the "Gedarene Maniac" under his arm; Dr. Bungle dangled "the herd of swine;" Dr. Buzz had the "immaculate conception" tied round his waist; and Mr. Graves had the "Resurrection" in his pocket. When the irons caught in a small tree, they whisked it off the ground, and, after making it describe a circle or two, dropped it flat; but finally, when the irons caught in an old oak, deep rooted in the earth, — a genuine tusk of Cerberus, — the balloon was speared in the side, and the world was deluged with gas.

"Thus collapsed Supernaturalism," said Mr. Hart, whereat Mr. Religious Life cried in loud voice, "Thus perishes preternaturalism or vulgar miracle-ism. The grand fruit on the Tree of Life has ripened on the husk of Revelation, as it has been given to the Greek, as well as to the Jew and to the Roman, and also to the Saxon. How mysterious the growth of the ear of maize! first the tender shoot, and then the fluttering flag, and soon the silk and the spool; and when the pollen has dropped, how skillfully the pearls are strung, and hidden in the green casket! Thus the growth of the Word! Every image is a casket, and the Truth is the pearls within. O mystery of mysteries, the unfolding of the germ and the transfusion of the gathering juices; of that which falleth into the ground and dieth, and also of that which is ground into the bread of Life! Deep, impenetrable, altogether inscrutable art thou; and the highest I can do is to wonder, wonder, and wonder again. Oh, woe to him who seeth naught in the inimitable art of God but the freakishness of that huge Leviathan called Nature! for he is blind to the things of the Spirit. But even I am blind to much that is. So let me grope on and on; and by and by I shall leave this cave on whose walls, as Plato tells, the shades of a Reality as yet unseen fall and flit ominously across my path, dim-lighted by the fires of my Passions, — but even here Imagination fails. And so, like Plato before me, I blend with the vacuity of my own words, and sink exhausted to die. Yes, even Plato had water, — word-water on the brain, — it put out his fire, — and it is well that he, in his Socrates, confesses that he knows nothing. But now, Reason herself is baffled, for Nothing is Death; and, since Death is not at all, there is no Nothing. Thus Affirmation recommences where I thought it ended, and I rise again out of the grave of words to reappear unto those who refuse to believe that Life Eternal is the inalienable possession of the Just. O joyful descent into Hell! thrice joyful transfiguration, and most glorious ascension, infinite as God, yet more incomprehensible than Evil! Thus I pray, having died in the word as I have died in the flesh, on the cross of Endeavor, on the cross of Prejudice, on the cross of Fanaticism, and on the cross of Virtuous Resolution, — a perpetual Jesus, an everlasting Prometheus, a wandering Jew, and a stationary Christian. But there is no reward for me but the good that I do; for, the moment I stoop to enjoy the fruit of my labor, I am again undone, and must be crucified afresh, and that by my own hand. So blame me not, my brother, for the poverty of the hope that I give thee, and for the hard task I would fain impose upon thee; for, verily, if thou doest not as I have done, do now, and will forever do, it were better for thee to go down this moment into the grave which is prepared for thee. Yet thou thinkest the yoke of Jesus was light; and thou preferest it to mine. But know that I, Religious Life, am the Saviour; and unless thou believest in me, in one or other of my manifold forms, thou shalt surely sink under the cross of the Devil, and I shall be crucified again in thy barbarous soul. Thus I go on my knees before thee, O vilest of the vile, and beseech thee, even as I tolerate thy Judas-kiss, to go and sin no more. Have mercy upon me, O world, and mock not with thy indifference, — thy vinegar and sponge, — the gift of Infinite Compassion."

# BOOK III.

## RECONCILIATION.

# I.

## A COUPLE OF MIRACLE PROTECTORS.

WE must apologize, O reader, for again bringing the Rev. Jehosaphat Pluffle into your presence; as we have no doubt that you must feel like the elder's wife when her husband brought home to tea a certain minister whom she detested. That good lady, being sent up stairs for the best Bible in order that family worship might be held, found, when she was returning to the parlor, Bible in hand, the said minister in the hall taking off his over-shoes, and, mistaking him for her husband, she brought the book of books down with terrific force upon his stooping shoulders, whispering savagely, "I told you, sir, not to bring that man here again."

Deacon Crisp and Dr. Pluffle sat at the breakfast table. The fair Miss Crisp presided. She did not look so bright as usual, nor was she so carefully attired.

The gentlemen were in the best of moods; for they had recently attended a grand conference of the Continental Miracle Protection Association which had been unusually successful. They were now talking about the immense amount of good which it had done in the world. What that good has been we have long tried to ascertain. We never could see anything in that miraculous institution but a sort of an Aunt Sally, established expressly for the amusement of infidels. For no sooner does it appear with a new version of the miracles in its pious mouth than the same is immediately knocked out by the irresistible missiles of Science.

"Upon my word," said the deacon, helping his guest to a fish-ball, "that was a splendid discourse of Dr. Scartippet the night before last. The foe had not a single leg left to stand upon. The objections of the spiritualists disappeared like dew before the sun. I was so delighted with the fine points he made that I spent two hours yesterday in hunting up a suitable present for him. Finally I fixed upon the largest Bible I could find, and sent it to him as a slight token of my gratitude. A dozen more like him in this wicked world of ours, and the millennium is fairly inaugurated."

"It was truly a wonderful discourse," said Pluffle. "For a surety it did justice to the Paulinian idea. I will trouble you for a little bit of mutton: fish-balls do not agree with me. I suffer a trifle from dyspepsia."

"I thought you were quite well now," said the deacon.

"Well, I can't say that I suffer so much as I used to. But I was just about to tell you, speaking of Dr. Scartippet that the great difficulty in the way of us miracle protectors is not so much the logic of the infidel, for that is beyond the reach of the masses, but his sacrilegious humor, and his irreverent jokes. But few will take the trouble to follow long arguments on either side. Our strength lies in our steady, long-suffering and persevering piety; theirs, in disgraceful mockery of sacred things. The Evil One has changed his tactics, and to-day his most destructive weapon is mirth. That is why," continued Dr. Pluffle, taking this opportunity to grind his own axe, with a sly look at Crisp, "I thought Mr. Lawson was not likely to become strong in the faith. His levity has cost me more than one serious thought."

"What you say is mostly true," replied the deacon. "The scoffer is worse than the serious skeptic. But I think your alarm about Malcolm is needless. He is truly light-hearted enough, and may have been a little profane. However, as he proved himself to be honest and sincere in other respects, I have great faith in him. He cannot resist the example of such lights as Rev. Oratone Buzz and Rev. Progressive Bungle; and Hezekiah Graves will have a most salutary effect upon him. Furthermore, the Lord is always with the honest and sincere."

"Not so!" cried Dr. Pluffle, putting his cup down so quickly that the teaspoon jingled in the saucer. "Spinoza, Parker, Emerson, and a thousand others, have been honest, and yet denied 'Him crucified' as vehemently as did Lucifer himself, and as skillfully. The mere morality of man, unless it is sustained by the recognition of Christ's merits, turneth to naught and has no weight with God."

"I must say I think you go a little too far, Brother Pluffle. I can't help liking an honest man, no matter what he believes, although I may sincerely deplore his fate hereafter."

"Oh, Mr. Crisp! do not shut your eyes to the littleness of man without the chastening influence of the Spirit. There is no good in us, — no, not any. What is man that thou art mindful of him?"

"Another cup of coffee, Dr. Pluffle?" asked the absent-minded Jennie, whose red eyes betokened the state of her heart.

Dr. Pluffle started at the interruption, and, after thanking her, resumed, "What has been the object of our labors and that of our beloved association of protectors? Has it been to strengthen mere human morality, or to defend the empire of the Lord? Take for an example that infidel, James Obstinate, residing in the next street, who turns John Locke into a Bible, and represents the class for whom we have done so much — why! he is, in a secular sense, a tolerably honest sort of man. What do you think he said the other day after I had drawn a touching picture of the infidel's death-bed?"

"What then?" replied Crisp.

"He said," resumed Pluffle, in a solemn tone, "Three times have I been on the point of death already: it gave me no concern whatever.' 'But were you not,' I inquired, 'alarmed in the least on the approach of the King of Terrors?' 'No,' he replied, 'far from that; I threatened to take him by the nose should he trouble me again, without purpose.'"

Here Dr. Pluffle looked round with an air of triumph.

"The ungodly rascal!" exclaimed the deacon sympathetically, thoroughly astonished at the hardi·

hood of the infidel, vividly recalling the moment when, frantic with fear, he besought the assistance of Malcolm on board the sinking steamer, while Jennie, remembering what Malcolm had told her about parrots, and acutely feeling the shallowness of Pluffle, who was so shocked at the idea of the King of Terror's nose, could not restrain a burst of laughter. The gentlemen stared at her in blank amazement. But the more fixedly they stared, the more she laughed. At last her father arose, and told her sternly that unless she showed more regard for his guest she must retire to her own room. Upon this she repressed her mirth, and in a short time they all resumed their meal.

Dr. Pluffle was discomfited. The idea of any one laughing where the King of Terrors was concerned! But then he had his favorite viand to console himself.

Before the meal was over the postman rang, and a letter was brought in and handed to the Deacon. "It is from Malcolm," said he as he opened it. Jennie turned pale and resorting to her handkerchief, kept her eyes intently fixed upon her father's face. He turned white and crimson alternately as he perused it. He rapidly reached the end, and was about to cry aloud, but, recollecting himself, he began and re-read it with the closest attention. Then throwing it across the table to Pluffle, he groaned aloud and said, "There is some mystery in that, Pluffle; for God's sake read that letter. It beats all. I never saw the like before. Resign not only his Redeemer, the salvation of his soul, but his girl here and all his prospects! What in all the world has come over him?" And the deacon glared wildly upon his daughter, who, unable to restrain her tears, left the room.  Dr. Pluffle read the letter aloud, and his eyes sparkled as he came to the choicest "infidel" bits and emphasized them.  It ran thus:—

Dear Sir,—

Love of Truth compels me to be frank.  I came here, as I said in the beginning, to learn the truth, and having, as I think, thus far faithfully performed this task,—except when, for a short time, I wickedly delayed this communication,—I acquaint you with the results of my labor. Please understand me.  I gladly affirm the fact of Revelation, as it has been given to all men, and to Christians in particular.  And I do not deny that the Orthodox Scheme of Salvation, as experienced by the believer, is true, as a scheme.  But please to dwell upon the word "scheme," for my idea hinges upon that. I see in your creed, intellectually considered, a design or contrivance to effect the salvation of man from all Harm or Evil, but no more than that.  Language is the garment of thought, and creeds are clothes of religious ideas; and, since I experience the painful fact that your creed no longer suits the mind of man,—for even the sanctity of its letter is violated flagrantly by progressive ministers,—I prefer to think out a creed for myself, or to weave a garment for my own religious being.  My spirit, as it were, has gone through a key-hole, and left its cloak behind.

Men re-act against the ideas of their innate deviltry, and refer all goodness to themselves rather than to God; hence the egotism of the radicals, whose great guns levelled against the popular theologies blow them to fragments; and hence, indeed, the mental restlessness of the age, which seeks relief in Romanism, ritualism, dilettanteism, sectarianism, and in the most decided infidelity to all that smacks of Divinity.

For my part, I have to say that my faith in the Eternal Providence of God remains unshaken; and such is my egotism that I seek to identify myself with him in every particular. Thought, however, even the thought of God, is nothing unless it is realized in living acts, and for this reason I renounce metaphysics and theory, save in so far as they spring from the spontaneous activity of my own mind, which I place under the curb of a universally acknowledged moral will. To this end, namely, to the palpable realization of the best ideas, I become an artist, and see no end to the improvement before me. Jesus to me still remains one of the grandest thoughts of Deity, but, mark you, only a thought, for do not we ourselves possess the gift of Eternal Providence? and it were mere idolatry in us to make Jesus other than the man he was. And in regard to his vicarious atonement, it is obvious that that is simply the doctrine of our common duty, namely, *infinite self-sacrifice* for the good of others, with whom our own welfare is inextricably bound up. But I need say no more than this: it is my unalterable conviction, arrogant as it seems that unless the Christian Church adopts the simple idea which I, a poor student, now faintly forecast, she will be swept away like a house that is built on the sand. Thus reconstruction, intellectual reconstruction, or radical reform, becomes my aim, and I now conclude, hoping to receive your approbation, and. in time, to clear myself of all chaos and obscurity. In sympathy with all religious activity,  MALCOLM LAWSON.

The deacon was quite puzzled by the above. However, he saw enough to assure him that Malcolm was anything but *sound*, in his favorite sense of that word. And he felt sick at heart; for he really loved the boy. The warm sincerity of the letter touched his heart, and made him think deeply, while Dr. Pluffle — his eye gleaming with an evil light — began : "I told you so, Brother Crisp. Honesty, mere human honesty, is no safeguard against infidelity. He has gone the road of the rest. Oh, this impious and godless age! How thankful we ought to be that the blessed little band of the Continental Miracle Protection Association remaineth to illuminate the straight and narrow path that leads unto salvation. Let us pray, O brother in the Lord, for this erring youth, who knows not what he does, who has eyes to see and yet does not see, who has ears to hear and yet does not hear."

Deacon Crisp did not open his lips. He appeared wrapt in deep thought. Dr. Pluffle wondered at his silence, but kept on: "Many are indeed called, but few are chosen. Let us renew our efforts to lead the erring into the right path."

"Ye blind guides!" ejaculated the deacon, who was still immersed in thought, without looking up and in an absent manner, as if he knew not what he was saying.

"What!" exclaimed Jehosaphat Pluffle, opening his eyes wider with astonishment.

"I was only reflecting if the lad might not possibly be right after all. When we come to think of it we have not made much headway in the last decade, notwithstanding all our efforts in the good cause. He is a most extraordinary youth. House built on the sand! No, it is not likely, — what am I saying? likely! no: it is not possible that the blessed system should have been built upon fraud, and yet infidels are honest men, and the church is divided and has made some mistakes. I confess it is beyond my comprehension. I never was puzzled so in my life before. I wonder what the rascal, — no: what am I saying? he is not a rascal, but a fool — has been writing to her all this time. I must look over her letters; it is possible that he may have injured her faith."

"Depend upon it, Mr. Crisp," said Pluffle with ill-concealed anxiety, "he has done all in his power to make a proselyte of her. Investigate, brother, investigate: a little poison is often fatal."

"The poison of honesty," muttered Mr. Crisp, who had resumed the reflective attitude, hardly conscious that he was speaking.

"No, I mean the infidelity," explained Pluffle in a lower tone.

"I tell you what it is, Pluffle!" cried the deacon with a sudden acquisition of energy, "what the boy says is worth looking into. What he says is not mere talk. He is not altogether a fool. The wisest of us are liable to error. I shall not decide in a hurry. We may exaggerate the importance of the C. M. P. A. I never dreamed I should find the honestest man I ever met in my life, not only outside the Independent Spirit Navigation Denomination, but an infidel into the bargain. We really must take a broader view of things. Lawson does not deny religion itself."

Pluffle sighed dismally, and attempted to reply in quivering tones, "Poor, weak human reason,—"

"Confound your poor, weak human reason!" thundered the deacon, firing up: he was in no mood for mere palaver. "I never thought you had any to spare, although I have always respected your faithfulness. Here is pious stupidity on one hand, and infidel brains on the other. I find it hard to choose between you."

As Crisp was not entirely void of insight into human nature, especially into those characteristics which he shared in common with his pastor, the latter's penchant for his daughter had not escaped his observation. He was at once vexed and irritated, disappointed and grieved, by Malcolm's avowal of his radicalism; and he required a more effectual palliative than the sops of scripture which Pluffle offered to his inflamed spirit. He also felt humbled in the sight of his minister, as he had always declared his confidence in the discrimination of the lad. Add to this the fact that he really had at bottom a certain regard for "poor human reason," which the logic of his creed had taught him to repress, if not to extinguish entirely. Malcolm's letter had roused it into action; and naturally, like a person whose temper is not improved by being disturbed during a sound sleep, he visited his ire on the first person who happened to be in the way. The high moral tone of the letter instantly kindled in him the conviction that man was not so bad as he was in the habit of calling him, and in the fitful light of this conviction he caught a glimpse of his own worldliness, and especially of Pluffle's. Then his own love for the boy, and the prospect of another quarrel with Jennie, were not without influence upon him. He was, in short, fairly bewildered, — nay, furiously so, and he spoke out of the fullness of his bewilderment. Pluffle was quite overwhelmed by the above outbreak of his beloved friend. He nearly lost his wits. However, he soon gathered courage, and was about to make a forcible reply, when it occurred to him that it might be more politic to notice the affront in a quiet way. Accordingly he arose with an injured air, and, bidding his dear brother in the Lord a cold good-morning, he left the room and the house and the stage of this story forever. If the reader has any desire to see him again, he will be under the mournful necessity of going to a prayer-meeting in the good city of Bragville.

The deacon was so absorbed by his own feelings that he scarcely noticed the departure of Pluffle. But soon realizing the stillness of the room, his conscience at once smote him for having cast a slur on the sacred cloth. Yet he managed to appease it by the words, "I guess it won't hurt him much. He'll get over it in a few days. Had it not been for my aid he would never have been a D.D." His moral sense now being in an unusually active state, this ignoble thought brought up his own and Pluffle's worldliness again, and he involuntarily compared the latter with Malcolm, whose integrity and spirited independence drew from him, in defiance of his theological prejudices, an exclamation of unqualified admiration. In this mood he lifted up the letter again, and as he re-read it with increased attention his anger fled, and the tears actually came into his eyes. His heart warmed still more toward the boy who had saved his life at the imminent peril of his own, even while his creed exhorted him to beware of the Fiend of radicalism. The tempest of his feelings at last broke loose in prayer, and he prayed audibly and fervently that light might be given him to guide him aright in this most important matter. But, alas! To many the Almighty is an overshadowing, an omnious gloom, not an ever-radiant luminousness, full of cheerful sympathy. Yet the two ideas are necessary, and the more perfect capacity will contain both properly balanced, the one against the other. Mystery is a zest to the best Intelligence.

It is reserved for religion to see God face to face. Theology, if it cannot correctly be said to see God back to back, at best catches a scanty glimpse of his shoulders.

How many indeed exist yet but half alive, bear-like throughout the winter of their idle discontent, in the hollowness of a narrow conventionality, or of pedantry and other artificiality, until the gleams, or it may be the steady glow of some sun-like mind, rouses them into charitable activity of some kind! Poor Crisp! if thou hadst even begun to appreciate the sublimity of the man whom thy superstition has dubbed Omnipotence, it had been much better with thee long ere now. Know that thou canst not simultaneously worship God and Mammon without growing in ear as much as in grace and respectability. Rich, active, but stupid and blind, art thou, even as was the fabled king of antiquity who abused the god-sent gifts of thrift and enterprise; and all the incidental charities that an unwelcome fate extorts from thy heart avail thee but little. How much better would it have been, hadst thou given a small portion of the great energy which was devoted to the protection of the miracles of the past, and to the filling of thy purse, to the grander miracle of thine own being, so that thou couldst profit by the hour that is, the Eternity that is daily proffering itself to thee. But even thou hast not lived in vain for thy kind. Thy ant-like spirit has been productive of much good, notwithstanding its auricular adornment, in that thou hast helped build in the western wilds cities of many minarets, scored the continents with railroads as if with an iron pencil, stitched them together with magnetic wire, and studded the seas with golden prows and snow-white sails. Yet of what good all these marvellous works of skill, if nobility and integrity of purpose keep not pace with their construction and government? For a verity, if these elements be wanting, they only add to the weakness of the weak, to the evil of the evil, to the diffusion of that whose safety is in limitation to the spot of ground that has given it birth. Happy is he who escapes the taint that is in the moral atmosphere of the times. Every social commotion wafts it into our homes, and there is no end to the tribulation it prepares for us. We can almost see it gather and grow like the cholera cloud, hovering gloomily over our monuments and domes, so that the danger of contagion is greater in the so-called sanctuary than within our own doors. It would seem that the Almighty intended from the beginning to grow many a worthless crop of animal life that he might plow it under for the sake of the harvest that is to come. It is a matter well worthy of note that so much more attention should be given by the present generation to the increase of luxury, to the mere titillation of the body, and to its meretricious adornment, than to that which we all, radical and conservative, Christian and Antichristian, openly acknowledge to be our nobler part, — namely, the mind.

## II.

### DEACON CRISP AND HIS RESOLUTION.

THE deacon was in a dilemma. For the first time in his life a faint sense of the insufficiency of his vast possessions to satisfy all wants came over him. He fancied at first that Malcolm was slightly insane, and naturally trembled at the thought of giving his daughter to him on that account, apart from any theological considerations. But the honesty shown by the youth was something that he could not reconcile with the impression that he was a "little out," as he expressed it. His moral sense strongly inclined him to forget creed and take him to his hearth again. Yet how could he do so in justice to his sacred convictions? In point of fact, he was situated like Malcolm himself, when unworthy considerations sought to turn the latter from the straight way. The real difference between their respective positions was that Malcolm's scruples were founded on regard for what he knew to be the truth, while the Deacon's were founded upon the dictates of mere habit and superstition.

"To give him my daughter," said the deacon to himself, "is to confess that I have misspent my life in so far as I have sought to sustain certain doctrines, — to proclaim to the world that the Continental Miracle Protection Association is the epitome of all foolishness. Paradox of paradoxes, an honest scoffer, a faithful unbeliever! The thought drives me wild." Here he had to clench his fist and cry, " But I shall not yield to the weakness of the moment. It grieves me to the heart, not only to disappoint my child, but to send him adrift; for I began to look upon him as my own son. Yet if thy right eye offend thee, pluck it out and cast it from thee ; for better it should perish, than that thy whole body should be cast into hell. But has he really offended me or Heaven to that extent, or is it my doctrines that have offended us all? Alas! alas! I am very weak, and all is vanity and vexation of spirit. The Roaring Lion has prevailed against him, and stolen him from the fold. But then he is honest, and the pleasures of the world seem to have no attraction for him ; for he throws them back to me as if they were handfuls of orange-peel. There surely is something in him."

But Mr. Crisp's principal devil, Dr. Pluffle, had been cast out, and his natural piety rose above debasing superstition. Shortly after Pluffle went he arose with a weary air, and he sought the apartment of his daughter with unsteady steps, for the deacon, owing to his intense application to business, had been somewhat out of health of late years. He found Jennie reading quietly, all traces of her late emotion having disappeared ; and she arose with a smile to receive him. But he was now so filled with the sense of his dignity as a guardian of the Faith, that he could only frown.

" I am here," he began, in severe tones, "to talk to

you about Malcolm. Oh, Jennie, when did this fatal change take place in his religious sentiments?"

"But a few days ago. I could not bear to tell you. My heart was crushed at the thought of your grief. But do not misjudge him, father; he is honor and justice both."

"But, my dear child, he is a heretic; just consider,— a heretic open and defiant; an apostate to the Church; a rejector of Him crucified; and yet you, my daughter, step out of the inner temple to become the prey of the Christless. God have mercy upon us! I pitied a frozen viper and thawed it out on my own hearth-stone. Behold what has happened!"

"But, father, dear, dear father," she cried, as if possessed by a new spirit, "that is palpably untrue; Malcolm is the saviour of your life, not you of his, and never before has he had more of God than now. The opposite of the viper, it is he that strives to warm you into new life; yes, you, O my father, who have allowed such as Bungle and Pluffle to freeze you unto blindness! Malcolm a viper? No: he is the sun, and those men are the vipers."

"You are mad, child, quite mad," gasped the deacon, with more doubt as to the truthfulness of his position. "Your lover is the victim of pride and sophistry, and you are naturally the echo of his thought."

"He is not 'the victim of pride and sophistry,' but he is a seer of the simple Truth. And what though I do echo his thought, is it not greater than mine and stronger than the world? I love him because he is true to himself; and if this be madness, why, madness is the blessing of God."

"'True to himself,' that is a very vague expression. 'True to the Master,' is the right word."

"Yet the prodigal,— did he not come to himself before he returned to Forgiveness?"

"True, my child, true; but that is a mere idiom, meaning the return of thought to a thoughtless person."

"Thought, then, must be but a small matter to you, father. To Malcolm it is everything: the surging sea and the green earth; the sun and the stars; even God himself; and not only me, but all that is yours and mine he spurns rather than be untrue to it. Can you gather grapes of thorns or figs of thistles, or receive from the darkness the crown of light? Malcolm has given me new hope, new life, and shall I at your command give it up again? No. He is mine and I am his, and the Church herself shall perish before we are torn apart."

"O Jennie, my only child," he replied, plaintively, closing his eyes as if he had tired them looking out into the night, "I do not understand it. I do not understand it. You are both Christless, yet you are not Godless; you are both lovers of Truth, yet given up to Heresy; both the most faithful of children, yet rank infidels. Oh, take the dust from out of my eyes. What fatal spell baffles my tongue and cramps my intellect to the mockery of all speech?"

"Think again father, and again," she cried, "with the aspect of a Judith in the tent of Holofernes, sabre in hand. It is very simple, oh, so simple, a child is equal to it. Infidelity is faithlessness; and if you can show me aught that he is faithless to, unless to faithlessness itself, I will rank him with the plague, and call him King of Evil."

"Enough, enough, you have said enough! Every word is a sharp sword. But you must winnow your grain of Truth of bushels of chaff. If I depart from the letter of revelation, which ages and ages of philanthropy have sanctified as the holy of holies in the Temple of Truth, an abiding place of God, whither shall I flee for refuge? Endless doubt and tribulation storm in upon me, and send me forth like King David in the night to mourn the rebellion of my blood. Alas! to think that I, in my old age, should be torn from my kingdom of the Cross and be swept away by a tide of infidelity, pouring from the breast of my only child. Help me, O Christ, to be true to thee in this hour of peril, and I shall not sink as one of little faith. Jennie, you are wrong, you must be wrong; the Bible cannot lie."

"But Pluffle can — and the rest. Would to heaven they were all swamped by the same infidelity! See to it, father, and guard well your eyes. The dust of superstition is worse than that of atheism, and the service of Mammon is the leprosy of the Christian as well as of the Jew. As Malcolm has helped me, so may he help you."

"Give me time, time, and I will penetrate this mystery. Now I am tired, quite tired; a glass of wine, child."

Here the spirit of Judith vanished, and Jennie was herself again, — all tenderness, — and she ran to serve the old man.  But, in another moment, she, too, experienced reaction, and she sank exhausted on a chair.  Then it was that her father felt his heart change, and he approached her full of sympathy.  Almost forgetful of his Faith, he promised to recall her lover.  But scarce had he done it, when he regretted his haste ; for he fancied still a resemblance between himself and Peter, when he denied his Master before the judges of Israel.  Yet he wrote to Malcolm to come without delay, as his heresy was overlooked in part, on account of his integrity, which permitted the deacon to hope that there still remained a chance of salvation.  The young man wondered a moment, and then went to bid Shaft good-by.

## III.

### ADIEU.

> "Grau, theurer Freund, ist alle Theorie,
> Und grün des Lebens goldner Baum."
> —*Faust.*

MR. SHAFT was a constant mystery to Malcolm. That gentleman, radical as he was, could preach in many pulpits, and that without sacrifice of self-respect. His was the rare genius of agreement, and where most people saw chaos and confusion, he perceived a measure of light and order. Endowed with singular energy and fixity of purpose, he seemed to occupy a high seat in the house of knowledge, whence he serenely surveyed the spectacle below. Yet he was not without the impulse of a passionate nature. He could asseverate with startling emphasis that he was quite right, and that all others were only measurably so, and if the Universalist had not already killed the Devil, he would certainly, with fell intent, have thrown not merely an inkstand, but himself, at his head. He was never the same to Malcolm since the latter's obvious but temporary aberration, and he did not omit to speak his mind on the subject. But the contrition of the youth softened him somewhat, and he began to forget the untoward circumstance. "Do not, Malcolm," he said, " flatter yourself that you can ever *be much* after what has taken place. You are no longer a fit temple for the Spirit's permanent abode: the best you can now do is to prepare for his chance sojourn."

"But work will work miracles with the worst," cried Malcolm, with an anxious but confident look. "It is true that I turned my back to the sun, and began to flirt with the moon ; but realizing my folly, I return to the light. She welcomes me as if I had always been true to her."

"You are in luck, surely. A fortunate fluke in most games will cheat skill himself and pocket the stakes. But it is otherwise with the game of spirit: there the reward never exceeds the merit. Affirm and you will be affirmed. Deny and you will be denied. Do you think the Eternal Yes, as represented by Jesus, could ever have been uttered if it had not been lived ? In it behold the grand affirmation of nineteen centuries. Goethe knew that he could not write better than he himself was. Hence the negative character of " Faust," which is but a fit symbol of the present time. Nothing but the realization of the weakness of my own character prevents me from aspiring to the dignity of the true preacher who is really a prophet, a divine person who comes to give us new form and life. Thus far the pages of history are full of the doings of One. And the so-called ministers of His word are little more than the sextons of His church. In spite of myself, being far inferior to Him, I am drawn into the maelstrom of his influence, so strongly indeed, that I belong to that church whose Realized-Ideal, until it is superseded by a better, shall remain supreme."

"But do you not thereby sacrifice your individuality?"

"Yes, in the worst sense of the word. After all, personality is not individuality. I exchange the one for the other. Individuality, however strikingly characteristic of the person, is only that whereby he is distinguished from others. Jesus and Judas, as individuals, are alike distinguished, the former for goodness, and the latter for badness; but as persons, Jesus partakes of Divinity, while Judas is hardly worthy of the name of person. To me, therefore, individuality is the direct negation of the Universal, the genius of disagreement, the Darkness, which, despite his seeming terribleness, is condemned to flourish but an impotent sword in the face of all-conquering Light."

"Impotent! that is just what I cannot believe. All the Philosophy in the world cannot keep me from seeing that palpable hurt, Positive Evil, actually exists. Look at his ravages in my own heart. And so obvious is the destruction which attends every stroke of his death-sword that I wonder why clergymen can talk so coolly about it. The trials of men are not the angels of God. Good Heavens! why can't people see that the Father of Lies is simply the Father of Fools, and have done with him? This miserable, self-delusive, optimistic soothing is little better than snake-charming. It has done me so much harm that I often feel like asking God to make me a fiery serpent, and cast me hissing into the midst of his enemies. I hate your *splendid speaking* and theological refinements while so much remains to be done for the moral life of the country. Why regale fraudulent traders and dishonest politicians with the sweets of optimism in the presence of a *supremely just God?*"

"Keep your temper, Malcolm, and let the dead bury their dead as they best can. Let us continue with the intellectual or rather ideal aspect of things, which we all have in common. I was about to say," — and Mr. Shaft looked as if he rejoiced in his equanimity, while Malcolm subsided at once, — "it is wrong even to name or denominate ourselves, as apart from our fellow-men. Sectarianism is the worst feature of the times."

"But are we not all aiming at the broadest platforms?"

"Yes; but most indirectly, and with only half a heart. Instead of acting on the principle of essential unity, — namely, that we are really one in honest motive and desire of betterment, — we are too apt to rest on the assumption that those persons who will not share our belief seek only their own Good at the expense of their fellow-men. But I am strong in the faith that we all love the Good, each after his own fashion, according to the extent of his Universal Light. And as the Good is only conceivable in and by the Person, how can we avoid striving to realize Him in ourselves; and indeed, from the intellectual point of view, I see nothing to retard that realization but want of unanimity in the acknowledgment of the Ideal State."

"Acknowledgment of the Ideal State?"

"Yes, I mean what I say. That want of unanimity is represented by *isms*, and all other attempts at invidious distinctions and separate or individual existence. For my part, as I said before, I ignore them entirely, and recognizing the unity subsisting beneath all outward things, I aspire to the life of the Spirit, and that life is best expressed, if we speak about it at all, in the most correct language. How absurd it is to call the Good or the God that is in us individual; how impious and contradictory the term a holy or complete individual!"

"I hardly understand you."

"What! Don't you see that a man is only Divine in so far as he, rising above and descending below all separate existence, obtains the unity so strongly felt by Jesus in the holiest of his prayers. I will set no bounds to my soul, however marked the distinction which places me above or below the level of my race, but rather pour myself forth in sympathy with all persons, however great or small their so-called individualities. For my limited or individual nature, moral and intellectual, is neither more nor less than the old Adam, and the sooner I exchange him for the new the better."

"But do you not contract yourself in thus distinguishing yourself by the peculiar use of words?"

"Not really. For in view of things as they are, it makes but little difference how we illustrate our theme, provided that we do it well. Yet, as a would-be-representative of the Golden Age, I prefer, even at the risk of isolation, to use the most correct language that I can find. Due appreciation of personality, in the moral sense particularly, is the redemption of the race. It is that which points to the Infinite lying below the microscope, and to that which transcends the utmost range of the telescope. It is that which fills me with the majesty of the universe, and makes me sink back from attempting to penetrate its mysteries, quite baffled by the ineffable sanctity of personal existence. Not that I disdain the aids of Science, but so far as I am concerned he has been but little more than a mocking Mephistophiles. He has taken more than he has given. There," cried Mr. Shaft, and he lifted up Shakespeare's Tempest, " in that play of the Spirit behold more than can be threshed from twenty stacks of doctrinal works, for it contains the only true scheme of salvation. How magnificently hopeful the soul of Shakespeare! What are the *dramatis personæ* of this winged thing, but the various aspects of man's being in this world? In the banishment of Prospero, I see the alleged lapse of the soul from her original blessedness, and his banishment is parallel to the confinement of Ariel. The former is Wisdom personified, and the latter is Genius, the most subtle influence of the soul. Both inherit the island, which is but a fit symbol of the earth as it is now inhabited. Sycorax is Superstition, ever a *blue-eyed* sorceress, whose ministers, prevailing against Genius, imprison him in the cloven pine. Can't you hear him moan in the wooden hollowness of the scholastics? Wisdom alone is equal to his release, and, being released, he must serve him as long as he requires. For him he flames amazement, tells no lies, rides on the sharp wind of the north, does him service in the veins of the frozen earth, being in short a veritable Moses' rod. How infinitely successful the joint action of Prospero and Ariel! The calamity of shipwreck, like all evil, is only in appearances, for all the passengers and crew are saved. The virtuous man and woman, as represented by Ferdinando and Miranda, are now allowed to meet, and after — even under the present most favorable circumstances — being made to pass the ordeal of work and temptation, receive the blessing of the Gods. Dignity, Plenty, Peace, Hope are there to consecrate the holiest of unions. And the reconciliation of Prospero to his enemies follows as the natural end to this Divine Comedy; for this means the restoration of the tried soul to her former power and glory. Even Caliban,\* who represents the inferior

---

\* Mr. Shaft has, at least in regard to this character, as much Truth on his side as that aspiring evolutionist who has just written a remarkable book, intimating that Caliban is the missing link needed to complete Darwin's theory of man's progressive development from — I can't say what exactly, but, depend upon it, it is as near nothing as you can possibly get. However, the learned author has builded better than he knew. Caliban does connect man with worse than the ape, but as much now perhaps as ever; and there is no link missing in the chain of internal evidence to this effect. Coleridge defines Genius "as originality in intellectual construction, the moral accompaniment and actuating principle of which consists, perhaps, in the carrying on of the freshness and feelings of childhood into the powers of manhood." This is probably why so many great geniuses — great even as Goethe, from whom the modern idea of evolution seems to

man, or the Old Adam, cannot avoid coming to himself after he realizes the futility of rebellion against the best of masters. Mark the art of Shakespeare in taking him away from awakened purity in that he provides him with a suitable god in a drunken butler."

"But is he not indispensable as the earth herself?"

"True. But having brought the wood and lit his master's fire, let him go where he belongs. Genius and Wisdom can now do without his ministrations."

"And is Ariel nothing more than Genius?"

"Yes. He takes the part of Conscience, who is always a harpy to the bad, and thus shows the power of personality even in such as Caliban, to whom he gives the lie. Witness also his speech to the three men of sin. He compels Nature to rise in her might, and belch forth indignation at their crimes, and makes the ghost of their murdered Virtue drive them to sorrow and repentance."

"But you forget Gonzalo. Who is he?"

"The blind idealistic individualist who is always like a shipwrecked courtier on a desert island. He would, with such perfection, govern as to excel the golden age itself, yet cannot, for the life of him, do anything but talk about it. He stays content even with his materialistic associates, guarding his sleeping king, the type of weak inactivity."

"But is such an idealist really unpractical?"

"That depends on the *character* of his individual-

have emanated — are sometimes tempted to forget the presence of the Muse, for the sake of making dirt-pies with the lower classes of child-like persons.

ism. In so far as he is a genuine, a truly universal man, he exhibits in himself the golden possibilities of the future, and is therefore the most practical man alive. Yet, the trouble with him is that he allows the speech to stand for the deed. He forgets that the moral act is the first step towards the realization of the ideal state, which is in reality the millennium, the acknowledged golden age of Christianity. But beware of false prophets. That vision of the poet will never be realized until, through the co-operation of Prospero and Ariel, the Ferdinando and Miranda are produced, and, in the absence of Caliban, brought together. How fortunate that Sycorax is a blue-eyed hag! There seems to be everything in the simple, yet significant fact, that Mary, the purest of women, should still be worshiped as the Mother of God."

"There is more in Shakespeare than I thought there was. How strange if he should prove to be the coming man in whom we are all to be made alive!"

"Do not be irreverent."

"Pardon me. Please continue. Why should Prospero resign his books, and set his Ariel free?"

"That is the most beautiful part of it all. The Prosperity of this golden hour no longer requires their aid. Wisdom sees his task accomplished in the blissful union of his children, with whom he is in perfect sympathy. For, as you see, each personification in the fable represents an acknowledged aspect of the Whole Soul or the Complete Person in whom Ariel is finally set free. Thus Individuality perishes of its own accord, and we find, in short, that we all are

'Tempests' in a greater or less degree, each one of us having within, as personified without, our false and true friends, exilers, Calibans, quarrels, reconciliations, Ferdinand and Miranda, and so forth, all more or less fortunate in their complex activities. Let us, then, on the approach of that calm when we no longer possess the art to enchant and the spirit to enforce, be able to say that we, too, like the Highest Wisdom, have given our fullness to those whom we leave behind us. And furthermore, let the prayer wherein we, like Prospero, find relief, be that conviction of Divine Unity, that realized aspiration which is none other than Freedom herself. What is all earthly existence but the pastime of the Spirit! It fades and dissolves with the beholder's eye, yet reappears with all original splendor to the ever-radiant eye of God. I deny that I am such stuff as dreams are made of; and, filled with a thought sublime even as that which gave the 'Tempest' birth, let me repeat, '*Before Abraham was, I am.*' And this I say — it may be with only partial appreciation of its signification yet — with the same humility as when a child I worshiped the Person of Jesus, whom continents still unite to call Divine."

"But stop a minute, friend: you do not really intend to say that Shakespeare, when he wrote this play, had all this elaborate thought in his mind?"

"Of course I do. His mind was possessed by the spirit of the same philosophy, and it was so real to him that it took form in his thought as an imaginative play, without any conscious effort on his part, even as the parables of Jesus came to him. My mind, on the other hand, is so weak in its wings that it will not fly unless it is well spurred by Reason, and this is why I am condemned to this infernal prose."

"Without conscious effort, you say, the genius of Shakespeare gave expression to the thought of the Tempest."

"Yes; that is, without special effort — more than is required for a conversation like this. He had the truth, and gave expression to it precisely as it impelled him from within. That gas-light illuminates the apartment, and the sun lights up a number of worlds, and as the illumination of the gas and the light of the sun, so the word of the poet and that of the Creator of the universe. And herein lies one of life's great lessons: let the Son attend to his Sonship, and the light will take care of itself; but should he forget himself for a moment, in self-conscious concern for his light or the splendor of his appearance, just in that degree he loses strength and balance and becomes less luminous. The truly great man cares little for the accidents and effect of good being, but everything for good being itself. True faith is the tree, and good works are the fruit. It was beautiful in Jesus to say, 'Let your light so shine before men, that they may see your good works and glorify your Father which is in heaven.' But this thought would not have suffered had he also said, Let your light shine wherever you are, no matter whether men see your good works or not; for, come what will, if you emit any light it of necessity adds to the glory of God. We are altogether too fond of exhibiting the few sparks of intelligence we possess to require exhortation to show them off. Not that I would advise you to put your light under a bushel of diffidence or indifference, but seek to give light, even as the sun giveth his, without regard to self-glorification. Rest assured it is sufficient to shine with the light of Divine Intelligence; for, in spite of all shadow, we shall be effective in proportion to our worth, and not one whit more or less. I sometimes think that if Jesus had dwelt longer on such a view of the matter, he would not, perhaps, have been so hasty in declaring himself the Messiah of the entire race. By so doing he has closed the eyes of many of his people to the possible advent of yet a greater than he, of a more golden fruit on the tree of life. What cares the king of day for the genuflections of his idolators? He has too much to be."

"So you blame Jesus for allowing himself to be called the king of the Jews, and for rejoicing in the name of Christ."

"By no means. When one has doubled ten talents who blames him for not having twenty-one? Beyond a doubt, had Jesus lived a little longer, and continued to grow in wisdom and in the love of man, he would have taken less satisfaction in the worship of his followers, and cared less for mixing his individuality with the personality of God. To say the least, it sounds a little presumptuous for any person in the form of a man to say that none can enter the Kingdom of Heaven save through him.

Such language, together with that which indicates his identity with God, and his pre-existence with him before the world was, must have been particularly offensive to the orthodox Jews of his day. And it was sure to lead astray blind believers in him by causing them to confound the Particular with the Universal, so that the former in place of the latter was sure to become the object of their devotion. It is not the isolated phenomenon of Jesus that we should worship, but the Eternal Spirit, of whom every heroic life is the best revelation. God is the tree, and Christ is the fruit."

"But this does not prevent you from acknowledging that that mysterious being is the one person most worthy of worship among the sons of men?"

"No: for he would not be worshiped as he now is unless he had earned his place in the hearts of his fellows. He will remain in his present position of Divinity until he becomes superseded by a greater than he. He is the best image of God there is, although he was placed betwixt a couple of thieves, and made to blend his cry of divine sympathy with the shrieks of stolid guilt and pitiful remorse."

"Do you not attempt to take his place in thus venturing to criticise him?"

"No more than any theological whipster who claps him into the throne of Jehovah and there protects him with his quills, even as the Russian serf guards with pointed bayonet the person of his Czar. I tell you Christian people have not called themselves depraved for the last few centuries without some foundation; and, this being the case, it is likely enough that I, who have associated with them should not be altogether untainted by their communications. I humbly confess that I had a human father, so it is quite possible that I was not immaculately conceived. I own my weakness as an individual, while I glory in my strength as a person."

"That is strange language, Mr. Shaft. I do not care for your distinction between the person and the individual. It seems artificial in the highest degree, and although it may be serviceable to you as a technical form of thought, even as Fichte's 'ego' and 'non ego' were to him, it is not likely to find universal acceptance more than any other accidental speech bearing on spiritual being. He who can appreciate so nice a distinction will prefer some form of his own which he is equally able to invent for himself. However, it may be something to ascend so high and find in such words a key to unlock the mysteries of the universe. I confess myself much obliged. More power to your transcendentalism."

"O Malcolm, Malcolm, your power to satirize all things has been dearly purchased. You realize not how much you have lost for lack of habitual reverence and prayerful worship of the Supreme Being, as He shines through all men, making their eyes the windows of His Heavens. I appreciate, I admire, the dexterity with which you heat your iron in the fire of moral energy. But, alas! the back of diseased humanity is not so much in need of cauterization as of the application of gentler remedies. I fear you are not a holy man; and, mark well my words, you condemn yourself to perpetual strife with the enemies of God when you might. if you pleased, subdue them with much less sacrifice of spiritual life. But the die is cast. You will doubtless carry your cross until the final moment, when it will be clear to yourself, at least, whether you are really a king or merely one of the mocking phantasms of the times."

"You are not wrong in this estimate of me, nor are you quite right: you cannot tell all that passes within your own bosom, not to mention mine. Nor are you, in spite of my confessions, familiar enough with my past life to form an adequate idea of me. But, as it is, I thank you for your sincerity, and I am glad to escape so easily from the judgment-seat. Every day, I suppose you are aware, is a day of judgment of some sort. You, then, being my god for the nonce, I am infinitely obliged for the clear revelations from on high, not only in regard to myself, but about Shakespeare and the rest of them. Good by: I am off for the West."

"Stay yet a moment, Malcolm. Has Deacon Crisp recalled you, notwithstanding your infidelity to the popular theology?"

"Yes, but reluctantly enough. However, he intends to confer with me, and hopes my heart will not be so hardened as to reject the salvation proffered."

"And let his daughter go?"

"Yes: but it all depends upon her. She represents all that is good in him and his; and she is mine forever, in spite of Pluffle and Fate. I care not for the lucre which Crisp has piled heaven high, intending to die on the top and enter thus the joy of his Lord. But unfortunately he is more than two-thirds dead already. His life has gone with his love and there it is to be found. Methinks I see it turn into a snake with scales of emerald and gold, and drag its glistening length through thickets of thorns. What a terrible bush are those plains of Mammon! The skeletons petrify on the sands. Blessed Sol himself becomes a curse, and Earth, with parched hand, waves back the ghastly morsels prepared for her board."

"Yes, you are right, Malcolm. But even skeletons die; and herein, in the negation of negation, — two negatives make an affirmative, — in the death, so to say, of Death lies the hope of the worst. O thrice blessed optimism! Read Goethe's 'Dance of the Dead.' During the dance the warden stole the shroud of a particular ghost and hung it on the point of the steeple. The poor ghost climbed after it like a huge spider on the wall. But the moment the skeleton grasped his shroud the clock of the church struck one, and down he tumbled head over heels to his utter extinction. What an example of acquired Life, of the Ideal attained! The living body is but a chariot of fire, and when it has borne us aloft into the regions of pure-mindedness, it falls to the ground and flattens like the mantle of Elijah. The striking of the One is the attainment of God, and behold, it sends Death to the grave forever. The cock-crow but causes him to reappear with new vigor."

"Lucky skeleton, Mr. Shaft! Behold, I shatter,

shatter, shatter, and down on the pavement fall. Not even a grain of dust shall I leave behind. Good by, old bolt from on high. How fragrant the breath of the morning! See, she takes me in her hand, and now I sit on her wings. Good by, good by: I'll soon be far beyond. Have a merry heart. I shall come back with a lily."

So Malcolm left; but Mr. Shaft, in spite of his optimism, had not a merry heart, for he sang the song of the gas: —

"A student lay dying alone,
 And loud was the song of the gas;
'Thou singest,' cried he, with a groan,
 'Of her who lies under the grass.'

"'Ah me! she is gone,' was his sigh,
 'And left me to die in this room.
Has she gone to brighten the sky,
 To gladden the gate of the tomb?

"'To cheat me of Life that is mine,
 Or send me the Light that I craved?
God, give me the Strength that is thine;
 Without it I will not be saved.'

"The flame simmered low in reply,
 'I banished Queen Night from the room;
I threw but a glance from my eye,
 And down went her banners of gloom.

"'I chirrup and simmer and sing,
 And flirt with the fly and the moth,
And caper and flicker and spring;
 And light up the gems on their cloth.'

"'Whilst I,' cried this man who could see,
 'Am blind to all things but her face.
Alas! there is nothing for me
 But to leave this wearisome place.

"'A Spirit unbounded is mine;
 It ebbs at the thought of my bride;
But surges like seas as I pine,
 To rise on its fathomless tide.

"'A weaver of garments divine,
 I plied the most wonderful loom;
Yet she, with those children of mine,
 Was swept to a pitiless tomb.

"'O Spirit, rise higher with me,
 Or lend me the wings of a dove,
Yet leave in the depths of thy sea
 This ghost with the ghosts that I love!'

"'How foolish men are!' cried the elf.
 'I'm happy to praise my own name.
Rejoice in the light of yourself,
 You've got to go out just the same.

"'I rose from a billow of gold,
 And fled by the duskiest way,
To die in the gloomiest cold;
 But I'll laugh so long as I stay.

"'Yes, I, but a flame from the mill,
 Can caper and flicker and gleam,
While humans, the gods of the will,
 Are eager to die for a dream.'

"'To die for a dream!' is his moan,
  'It's not for a dream, but a death.
Their life has been only a groan
  From breast of Perpetual Breath.

"'No wonder I wither and die;
  Out, out is the light of my life!
Oh, what, at this moment, am I?
  An apple just halved by the knife.'

"The flame now distended its core,
  And lowered its beautiful head,
And faint were the rays on the floor,
  For the lonely student was dead."

# IV.

## A STORM.

MR. CRISP received Malcolm on his arrival in Bragville with evident kindness and respect, yet there was a something latent in his manner which Malcolm scarcely liked. It was, indeed, pretty obvious that the deacon was not likely to change for some time to come the prejudices natural to a person who had spent his life in advocating a fixed form of religion in favor of one which must appear to him loose and extravagant. Yet, as we said, he loved the boy, and, in consideration of the situation, was willing to tolerate his views; that is to say, if he kept them within the bounds of moderation. Moreover, he was not altogether without the hope that his prodigal son-in-law, that was to be, would soon realize the impractical character of his thought in view of the self-evident superiorities of Bungle and Buzz, the great luminaries of his church.

"My dear boy," he said, a week after his return, as Malcolm stood at the window looking out into the growing dusk with a melancholy air, "I have a private word for you; let me have your attention."

"Certainly, sir," said the youth, turning and placing his eager eyes full on the deacon's face. The deacon blinked; yet, recovering himself in a moment, he began:—

"While I admired the moral sense you displayed in speaking your mind as you have done, it has been a source of great uneasiness to me that you show no signs of appreciating the name of the Lord. But discretion, no doubt, will come with years, and whenever it does come, you may possess my daughter with my blessing and glad approval. In the meantime, however, I grieve to say that I, for my part, can neither honestly nor heartily give her to you. You see how it is. She has decided for herself; and, rather than begin a contest which would only result in misery for all, I do not impose my will upon her. Now, considering this state of affairs, you cannot expect that I will bestow upon her the means which, with the Lord's help, I hardly earned, that you through them may support and propagate your unholy opinions. You may continue to reside here in my house as her husband, where you will have facilities given you for study and research, comfort and amusement. But beyond this I can conscientiously do nothing for you, so long as you think as you now do in matters of religion, however much I honor the self-respect and honesty you have heretofore displayed. And, as to Jennie herself, it is my duty to let you know that she just now has nothing of her own, and will have nothing but what I choose to give her. Here, then, you know how I am to stand as far as you and she are concerned, as long as you continue to set your face against the revealed word of God."

"Dear Mr. Crisp," replied Malcolm, "you have relieved my mind of a great weight. I hated the thought and abhorred the act of coming to partake of the bounty of one who could not give it with a whole heart. Know once and forever that, in spite of the strong attractions, it is absolutely impossible for me to remain longer in your house than friendship requires. No, the Heavens will not fall. I love your daughter. Yes, I love your daughter even as I love my true self; yet not even for her sake could I so far forget myself as to exist under the conditions you specify. If I am to receive the gift of your daughter, I take her with a whole heart, and remember that she, being mine, must remain independent of those who have no confidence in her husband."

"But, my dear boy," said the deacon, anxiously, "be reasonable. Neither of you have any property of your own, nor are you likely to possess any, unless you meet with unexpected good luck. You see, in my house you will have everything you can wish."

"But self-respect. No, Mr. Crisp, I can wait yet a while. Present gratification is not that which I most desire; nor would I accept salvation itself on the terms prescribed. And, to tell you the truth, I am glad that we have come to this understanding of one another. I own myself deceived by the contents of your last letter. How could a radical enthusiast expect to find a father's love in a confirmed believer of your stamp? It is plain that I am not self-sacrificing enough to be worthy of you. You cannot tolerate me, and how can you presume that I will tolerate you? Alas! I know myself of old, and how bitter the memory! Adversity I gladly accept; it is much more congenial to me than prosperity. Yes, Deacon Crisp, I would rather go, for I have a great deal to do."

"What do you propose to do?"

"Preach the gospel to every living person."

"What gospel?"

"My own."

"Not Christ at all?"

"Only in so far as he harmonizes with me. He is an admirable illustration of the Wisdom and Love I aspire to preach."

"'Admirable illustration,'—confound your blasphemy!" roared the deacon, firing up; for the self-possessed irony of Malcolm exasperated him. "I tell you what it is, Malcolm Lawson, I see nothing for us but complete separation. Go, if you will, and take her with you."

"No, Mr. Crisp, I will not take her from her present home till I can give her one of her own; and that may be never, for I am a poor hand at money-making. Nor would I rob you of the pride and the greatest joy of your life. Keep her till I am able to do her the justice her talents and position require."

Here the deacon wept; and, throwing himself into a chair, gave himself up to the emotion of his heart. At this moment Miss Crisp entered and asked, in a tone of alarm, what was the matter.

Said Malcolm, "Jennie, it is not in the nature of things that your father and I can agree in that element of peace which would make my stay in his house tolerable for any length of time. He is, indeed, willing to give his consent to our marriage, but says he cannot do so as honestly and heartily as he would if I was more of a Christian. Moreover, he offers me, as a proof of his regard, his house for a home, there to remain, under his surveillance, dependent upon him for the bread I eat and the clothes I wear. That is impossible."

"It is not impossible!" cried the young lady, her blue eyes burning with the fire she inherited from her father; "you shall remain, and he shall do all in his power to make you stay, while we both unite to make you free as the air: for, at bottom, he loves you even as he loves me, and there can be no limit to his love. Do not be foolish, Malcolm, and make martyrs of us both to no earthly purpose. I declare to Heaven, and positively swear, that, if you go, I will go too, and work, if necessary, till my fingers bleed."

"Now, dear Jennie," replied Malcolm in the same serene tone as he replied to the deacon, "you cannot expect your father to have perfect confidence in one who seems to deny what he affirms to be essential to Eternal Life, and just consider what that mystic word means to your father. Life Eternal — Eternal, — and he has given his life, as he thinks, to secure this blessedness."

"I do not care what it means," cried the excited maiden; "I am tired to death of this word-mockery. Would you stab my soul with radical conceit, and sacrifice my life on the altar of your whim? Do you think that I will see honesty baulked, integrity impeached, and wisdom banished for all the creeds in the world? For shame, Malcolm, and you, too, father! Why should you allow contemptible differences to part you from that which you love most? What right have you, Malcolm, what right have you, father, after having come so near in your agreement, to say, Here are the limits of our love? Leave it all to Him who lives in my love for you both, and all will yet be well."

"Alas, Jennie," said Malcolm, "you take me away from myself. I love you, oh, how I love you! yet even as I love you I will do nothing which shall prevent me from loving you as a true man. Gladly, right gladly would I remain here, if I could in justice to us all. But there is work for me to do. Will it grieve your soul to know that I am about my Father's business?"

"But your Father's business is also my Father's business; and I will not let you go alone. You besought me to cultivate my will. I have done that, and you must take me as I am. I have said it, and go I will. I care not for wealth; your love is all I ask, and that I will have, in spite of the world."

Here Mr. Crisp, moved by this strange dialogue, arose, and, with outstretched hands, cried, "You are made for one another; foolish man that I was to try to part what God has joined together. I take you, Malcolm, to my heart, even as I have taken Jennie; and henceforth, I trust, we will bear with the infirmities of one another."

"Father Crisp, and you, Jennie, my bride," cried Malcolm, unshaken, "I thank you for your kindness, devotion, resignation, worship; but hear me once more: I dare not trust myself to stay here, all guarded, even as I would be, by the wealth of your combined affections. I am strong only when I am alone, far away in the wilderness of the world which I call mine. I will not stop to explain; my conduct and my work will explain themselves."

With a look of anguish, yet with a fierce lustre in his eyes, Malcolm waved a farewell to Jennie, and turned to leave, when a cry of despair fell upon his ear. It was from her. Poor child, this unexpected turn of affairs was too much for her, and, having cried aloud, she fell upon the floor as dead. Scarlet drops oozed from her lips, showing that a blood-vessel had yielded to the tumult within. This sad spectacle wrought an instantaneous change in Malcolm's mind, and he flew to take her in his arms, that he might give her relief, while her father tottered a moment, and then distractedly called for help, wringing his hands and reproaching Malcolm for his hardness of heart. We will not repeat what Malcolm said in this moment of grief and anxiety. Not till the physician had come, and given the assurance that, although Jennie had received severe internal injury, the chances were that she would be saved, did Mr. Crisp and he become themselves again. Then he said to the deacon, "In my despair I called you Jepthah. But what right had I to do it, when, in false exaltation of soul, I almost killed her myself. Good Heavens! where was my mind, or where indeed was common pity, not to say the sense which I boasted? Had we actually bent a couple of young trees into close embrace, and then, having tied her between, let them snap back, leaving her torn form to glut the vision of Moloch, we could not have done worse. But I was worse than you. In the jealousy of my soul, I had become my own Iago, and done with a speech the work of a pillow. Fool, fool, that I was! How could I, who strove for the highest, doom myself thus? Verily, had I killed her, a blight had fallen on my tree of life, and justly, too, for behold, murder was its fruit."

"Ah, yes, Malcolm, we have not been wise, but I will meet you more than half way: and hear me now. Satisfied with your purity of intention and wholeness of heart, I shall trust you henceforth, even if it is not given me to understand the peculiarities of your mind. I can well see that your nature is deep, so deep, indeed, that its roots, for aught I know, may extend to the bottomless pit. But such as it is, I cannot reject it at the frightful expense which is threatened, even to uphold the creed of my fathers. That, evidently, judging from the dissensions in the Church and the iniquity of its principal defenders, as seen in the late scandals, is doomed to speedy annihilation, and I, Thomas Crisp, am driven to confess it; for, to save my soul, I cannot see the sense of preaching redemption through Christ's merits, when mere boys like you and such as Bungle rely exclusively on their own. I must confess the whole thing far exceeds my understanding; but, whether or not, I began with Christ for my guide, and I have made my choice for all time. However, I am glad to find that there is still an honest man in the world, and repeat my assertions of entire confidence in you; for obedience to the ten commandments seems to be the object of your life. So I will not ask you to bend before my God, if you will but worship your own in spirit and in truth. In spite of myself, I love you even as I do my poor child there, and gladly embrace you as my own son; so pray let us forget in this act of reconciliation our mutual suffering for one another."

# V.

## A RAINBOW, THE TRUE LOVERS' KNOT.

"Now Israel loved Joseph more than all his children, because he was the son of his old age: and he made him a coat of many colors."

THE vicarious suffering of his daughter seemed to have made Deacon Crisp more thoughtful than ever, and he had several talks about religion with Malcolm, who, from the same cause, had become less combative.

"My dear Malcolm," said the Deacon with an affectionate look, yet in rather a formal manner, which indicated that he had a prepared speech to deliver (this was when Jennie was almost well), "the more I see of you, the harder I find it to separate your views from Christianity as originally taught by our Lord. In fact, if I dare trust my own judgment, you, when unbiased by your unaccountable hatred of miracles, do not say a single word against True Religion as I understand it. So, when I dwell upon this, and consider at the same time that your belief in a personal devil still remains unimpaired, I am loth to take a despairing view of your case. Now when a man, however radical in other respects, has the strength to hold on to the latter essential of the Faith, he is not so radically bad as some theologians maintain. Considering, then, this important evidence of latent orthodoxy together with your inviolate integrity, which is, no doubt, the result of careful searching of the Scriptures, I think it quite likely that the Rev. Messrs. Tightcreed, Lullaby, and Buzz would oblige me and kindly overlook your past and restore you to their lost confidence. I am just on the receipt of a note from Lullaby, in answer to one wherein I asked him and his brethren to exert their influence in your behalf. He informs me that the Church of the New Messiah is vacant, and his influence is not to be sneered at. Both Tightcreed and Buzz are under his thumb. But here is the letter, — see for yourself." And Malcolm took the letter and read aloud : —

*Dear Brother Crisp,* —     CHURCH OF SALVATION SURE.

I have to thank you for your kind letter, enclosing subscription for P. Bungle's defense, and asking me to recall the letter of excommunication which we, in the faithful performance of our Christian duty, sent to Mr. Lawson. I have to say, in reply, that, after due consideration and many prayers for Divine guidance, I, with Brothers Tightcreed and Buzz, will be glad to see your young friend once more — say the evening of the 1st of next month — in my vestry here, with a view to reconciliation. But please to remember, my dear brother, the untoward peculiarities of the young man, — his inordinate love of contradiction for the mere sake of contradiction, the abruptness of his style, the frightful ambiguity of his thought, and, above all, the dangerous egotism, not to say conceit, which vitiates his every thought and deed; but, since all his faults must be plainly visible to your illuminated eye, — an eye, indeed, which has rarely or never been deceived, — it is quite unnecessary for me to enumerate them. Yet, enormous and numerous as they are, it behooveth us to bear in mind that we are all included in that terrible fall from Blessedness, dating from the Garden of God; and, were it not for the light of the Son, those beams of perfect charity which enfold us in our falling state, giving each one of us the rainbow garment of Hope and Peace, we were nothing in ourselves. So, what I have to suggest at this moment is that, in Lawson's case, only the most fervent appreciation of the Divine Love, as manifest in the dear Saviour, can atone for his lamentable deficiencies. Now, if, on re-examination, he turns out to have this appreciation, and, at the same time, exhibits a conciliatory disposition, it is quite possible that I, with Brother Bungle's help, may prevail on Brothers Tightcreed and Buzz to assist at his ordination. Of course you are aware that the fact of disbelief in the miracles is a hard thing to overlook; yet there are many ways of making this painful disclosure. The Church, I am happy to say, is always charitable to those who speak with due regard to the religious sensibilities of her children; and if, as I advise, Mr. L. displays an amicable disposition, it will not be without effect on Brothers Tightcreed and Buzz, and their constituents.

Again: in regard to the merits of the youth, I side with you in respecting the tenacity of his thought and faithful adhesion to the principles of morality, while I cannot help admiring the aptness of his illustrations and the reach of his mind. Evidently there is enough in him to justify your anxiety to restore him to the bosom of his legitimate mother, the Church; and no doubt, if successful, you will not be without reward in a fairer realm. But, dear brother, let-me use the privilege of an old friend, and speak with the utmost frankness: *be on your guard lest you sacrifice too much for the sake of reclaiming one prodigal son;* although, be it said, there is more joy in Heaven over one sinner that repenteth than over ninety-nine that went not astray. Lawson has, indeed, much to do before he can fully justify his conduct to Christian people, for the infidelity of years is hard to eradicate; but if, through special grace from On High, he is permitted to follow your advice and mine, none of us will leave a single stone unturned to help him upward and onward. The Church of the New Messiah is vacant, and the public have more confidence than ever in our ministrations. What a pity that your protégé should have been the only one in our institution, except Mr. Ernest

Hart, who failed to appreciate the genius of Brother Progressive, the most brilliant luminary of our system! Yet, perhaps I am wrong to mention him in this connection, considering the thick cloud which darkens his fair fame. However, I shall take occasion to request your prayers for the bark which carries his good name. 'Tis true that it has risen "on hills of seas, Olympus high," but, alas, only "to duck again as low as Hell's from Heaven." But, O blessed freedom of speech and press, how can we thank thee for all that thou hast done to vindicate outraged innocence? Veritably, in this Christian period, when quackery and puffery are unknown, but a faint breath from thy lips is sufficient to dispel the storm, and save the ship of our love. For a surety, Brother Crisp, Public Opinion is a fiery sea; but is there not always a Saviour for the faithful? So let us return thanks to those kind angels of the Lord who have stood with our brother in the midst of the flames,—those flames which have been seven times hotter than ever before withstood by servant of Jehovah. Yes, Brother Crisp, I am happy to say that, as yet, not even the smell of fire pertaineth to his garments; nor is there a hair of his head injured, although many of his adversaries, especially those who launched him, have suffered severely. Is it not written, "Whoso believeth in me shall never die"? Thanks, then, to the Lord for his goodness, and to such as you, brother, who publicly announce your love and esteem for the great Progressive Bungle in this his great hour of trial. "Blessed are they which are persecuted for righteousness' sake: for theirs is the kingdom of heaven."

You will see, brother, from the above, that, owing to Progressive's unfortunate situation, I am left to be sole advocate in behalf of your radical protégé; but rest assured that I will do my best to meet your wishes, as well as Mr. Lawson's spiritual vagabondism will allow.

Yours in Christ,<br>
SIMON LULLABY.

"Dear Mr. Crisp," cried Malcolm, tossing the letter on the floor, "I am much obliged to you and Dr.

Lullaby. But please to know, once and forever, that I can have nothing to do with him and his associates. They are wholly opposed to my work in every sense of the word of God. Indeed it is not in the nature of things that I, notwithstanding my adherence to the personal devil, can consort with them. So it is quite unnecessary to re-open the book of my past experience. I fear I am dead to your church, in so far as it is represented by such as they, and it to me."

"But what do you intend to do, my dear boy?" cried the Deacon, testily, in a state of great excitement. "I certainly hate to ask you this question again, but I cannot see how to help it. So, for God's sake, let me know what you are going to do with your radicalism. What are you going to do with your radicalism?"

"To tell the Truth, as I conceive it, without regard to cost, and with all my heart and soul. I am preaching now, and I do not see how I can become anything but a minister in the original sense of the word. Is the merit of the prophet to be measured by tributes of popularity and applause? If so, your Lord, when he was most of a man, was nowhere; and the greatest prophets but fugitives in the desert, fed by ravens and strangers. Last night I preached, and the day before, and the night, too. In truth, I do not think I am good for much else."

"That's right, Malcolm. Keep yourself before the people, — keep yourself before the people. Your preaching is often good; and sometimes I catch myself listening, even against the whisperings of conscience. But if you do not wholly despise seculai promotion, there are other ministers in the Christian Church besides Tightcreed, Lullaby, and Buzz. What do you say to the Rev. Messrs. Faithful Performance, Common Duty, and Frank Declaration? Surely, your radicalism will not suffer by co-operation with them, even if they do belong to the Church. Their congregations, it is true, are not large; but, as everything must have a beginning, it will not do to ignore their existence entirely. Perhaps you might be induced to co-operate with them."

"O, dear sir! how can I express my gratitude? I have long sought a better acquaintance with those dignitaries of the Invisible Church, but found it hard work. They were so busy doing good to others, or engaged in self-improvement, that they had but little time to waste on one like me. But I had no idea that you were so intimate with them as to risk the introduction of so confirmed an egotist as I am. Pray do not hesitate a moment. My mind is open, and there is, I fear, a great vacuum to be filled by them."

"Spoken like a worthy son of the True Church," cried Mr. Crisp, with an excess of enthusiasm, "even if you are somewhat peculiar in your views. I have already sent for those clergymen, the companions of my boyhood, when I worked twelve honest hours a day for five dollars a month and board. They cut my acquaintance when I went into the railroad-bond business; and, depend upon it, I would not ask them hither, were it not for your sake. They will be here in three minutes, when we shall see what can be done for you."

At the time specified, the said gentlemen arrived. To the surprise of Mr. Crisp, Mr. Frank Declaration recognized in Malcolm an old friend in whom he had great hopes, yet, at the same time, he wondered to see him so intimate with Mr. Crisp; but, on hearing the circumstances, his wonder departed, and he expressed pleasure thereat. However, in answer to Mr. Crisp's request that he would use his influence to advance the material welfare of the youth, he was forced to declare that his influence in the Church was small. "Yet," said he, "such as it is, he shall have the full benefit of it."

Mr. Performance, on the other hand, was rather slow in coming forward with any definite offer of assistance; but this was to be expected in him, as he was not given to rash promises.

"Of late years," said he, "I confess, with pain, my influence among wealthy Christians has been wofully on the wane; and, unless Mr. Lawson possesses unusual merit, I can do but little for him. To be quite frank, I scarcely like his style. Here and there fatal weaknesses are discernible, and it is altogether too negative to benefit the cause of True Philosophy. Nor are his imperfections to be attributed to youth alone. Sin has lessened him by one-half of his natural stature, and the best half at that; but he knows what's the matter, and there is, after all, some chance for him. No doubt, with the active aid of Mr. Duty here, he will become a profitable servant. Yes, unmistakably, Mr. Duty is the man for him, and, if he endorses him, I have nothing further to say."